Carbon Shinai
カーボンシナイ

CF-Type
DB-Type
K1-Type
K2-Type

Orange Red Yellow

The official Carbon Shinai rubber stopper have been improved.

The NEW official rubber stopper
¥300 (Domestic price in Japan)

WARNING!!
Never use anything other than our official rubber stopper on your Carbon Shinai !!

When in use of your Carbon Shinai.....

1, To prevent injury, be sure to use our official rubber stopper. Do not use stoppers made for conventional bamboo shinai on your Carbon Shinai, as there is a risk of injury to your opponents if the tip distorts or the piece of shinai slips out from the rubber stopper and penetrates through their men-gane. (men grill)

2, When choosing a saki-gawa (tip leather), make sure that it is more than 5cm in length and completely covers the official rubber stopper. If the saki-gawa is shorter than 5cm, there is a risk of injury to your opponents if the piece of shinai slips out and penetrates their men-gane.

3, Whatever the reason, do not shave the surface or cut the length of your Carbon Shinai. If you shave or cut, the Carbon Shinai will get damaged to result in injury to your opponents.

4, Always check the condition of the surface of your Carbon Shinai before, during and after use. As soon as you notice any damage, stop use of the shinai immediately. There is a danger of injury to your opponents if your Carbon Shinai gets split or broken.

5, When tying the naka-yui (leather binding), either tie a knot in the tsuru-ito (cord), or tie one end of the naka-yui to the tsuru-ito, or by another means ensuring that it does not move up and down during use. If there is any damage whatsoever to the saki-gawa, tsuka-gawa (hilt), rubber stopper, tsuru-ito and so on, replace them immediately with new ones.

6, If the tip of the Carbon Shinai get damaged, or a slat is protruding out of the saki-gawa, there is a danger that it could penetrate your opponent's men-gane and injure them.

Kendogu Revolution

Mu-Jun Men
武楯面

WARNING!!

1, Under no circumstances should organic solvents (such as thinner, alcohol, benzene, toluene, acetone, gasoline, kerosene, etc.), acidic or alkali chemicals, domestic cleansers, car cleansers, or anti-mist sprays, be used to clean the shield. These substances will cause the shield to deteriorate, leading to clouding, cracking or breaking, thereby resulting in danger of injury to the face.

2, Should the shield develop deep scratches or cracks on either the outer or inner surface, discontinue use of the shield immediately, and replace it with an undamaged shield. If the shield is used in such a condition, there is a danger of its breaking, causing injury to the face.

3, It should be fully understood that, as with the traditional Japanese Kendo-Men (mask), there is still the danger of injury to the face through fragments of broken bamboo or Carbon Shinai pieces penetrating through areas not covered by the shield.

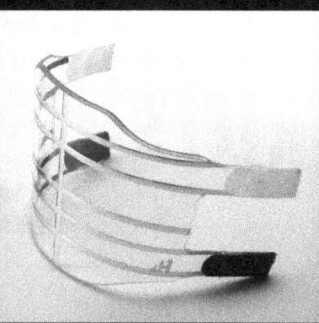

SG-Type

- SCIENCE TO SEEK SAFETY -
HASEGAWA
HASEGAWA CORPORATION

WEB : http://kendo.hasegawakagaku.co.jp/
Email : contact@hasegawakagaku.co.jp

Carbon Shinai — Points to be checked

DANGER !!   Before these happen.....   **ATTENTION !!**

Although the Carbon Shinai is much more durable than conventional bamboo ones, it will inevitably be broken since it is a Kendo sword which is beaten hard and thrust over and over again. Inspect the condition of the surface, sides or reverse of the Shinai's pieces before, during and after use, and stop use of the Carbon Shinai immediately should the damage like the following pictures be observed. (The pictures are just one examples of many.)

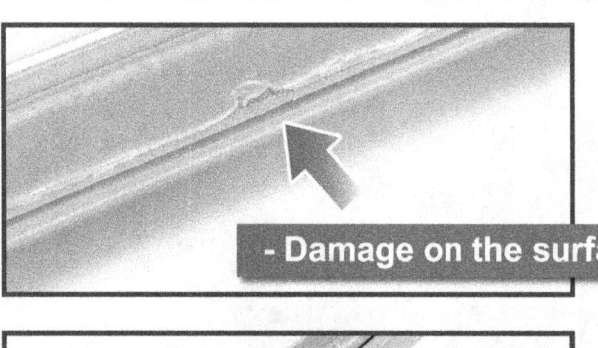
- Damage on the surface

- An unglued surface sheet

- Exposure of the Carbon fiber

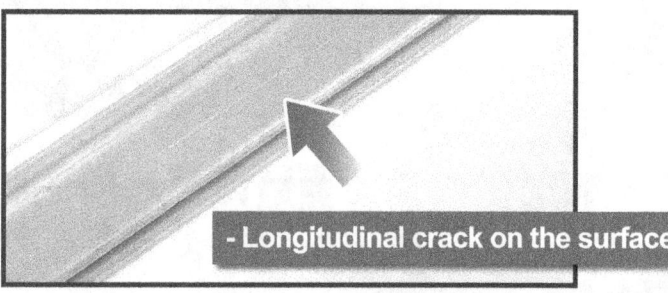
- Longitudinal crack on the surface

- Damage and ungluing of the surface

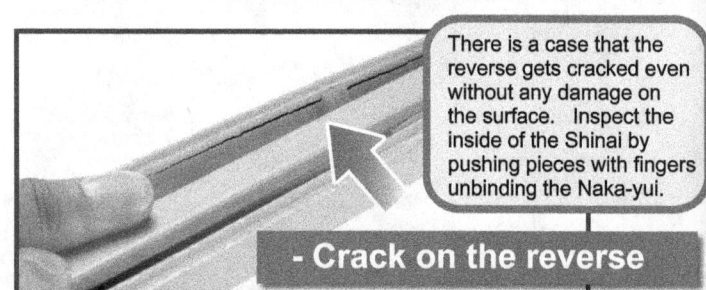
- Crack on the reverse

There is a case that the reverse gets cracked even without any damage on the surface. Inspect the inside of the Shinai by pushing pieces with fingers unbinding the Naka-yui.

HASEGAWA-KOTE

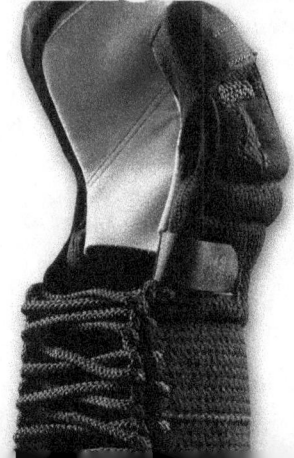

- Detachable and washable "Tenouchi" is easy to wash and dry.
- "Tenouchi" is replaceable when it torn. No need to repair.

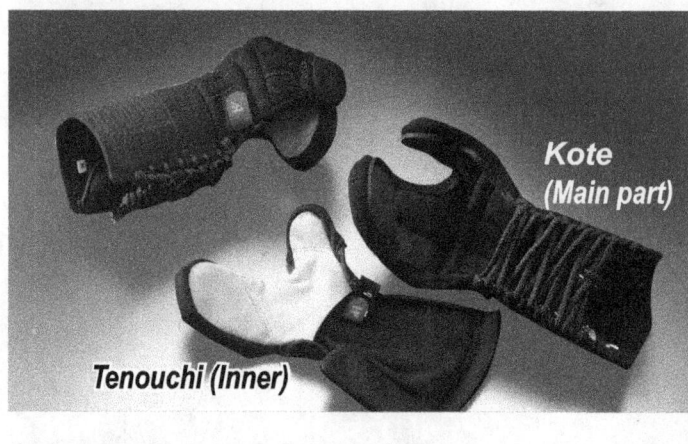

Kote (Main part)   Tenouchi (Inner)

- SCIENCE TO SEEK SAFETY -

HASEGAWA

HASEGAWA CORPORATION
http://kendo.hasegawakagaku.co.jp/

... Custom Made with Delicacy and Pride

In Japan.

www.chibabudogu.com

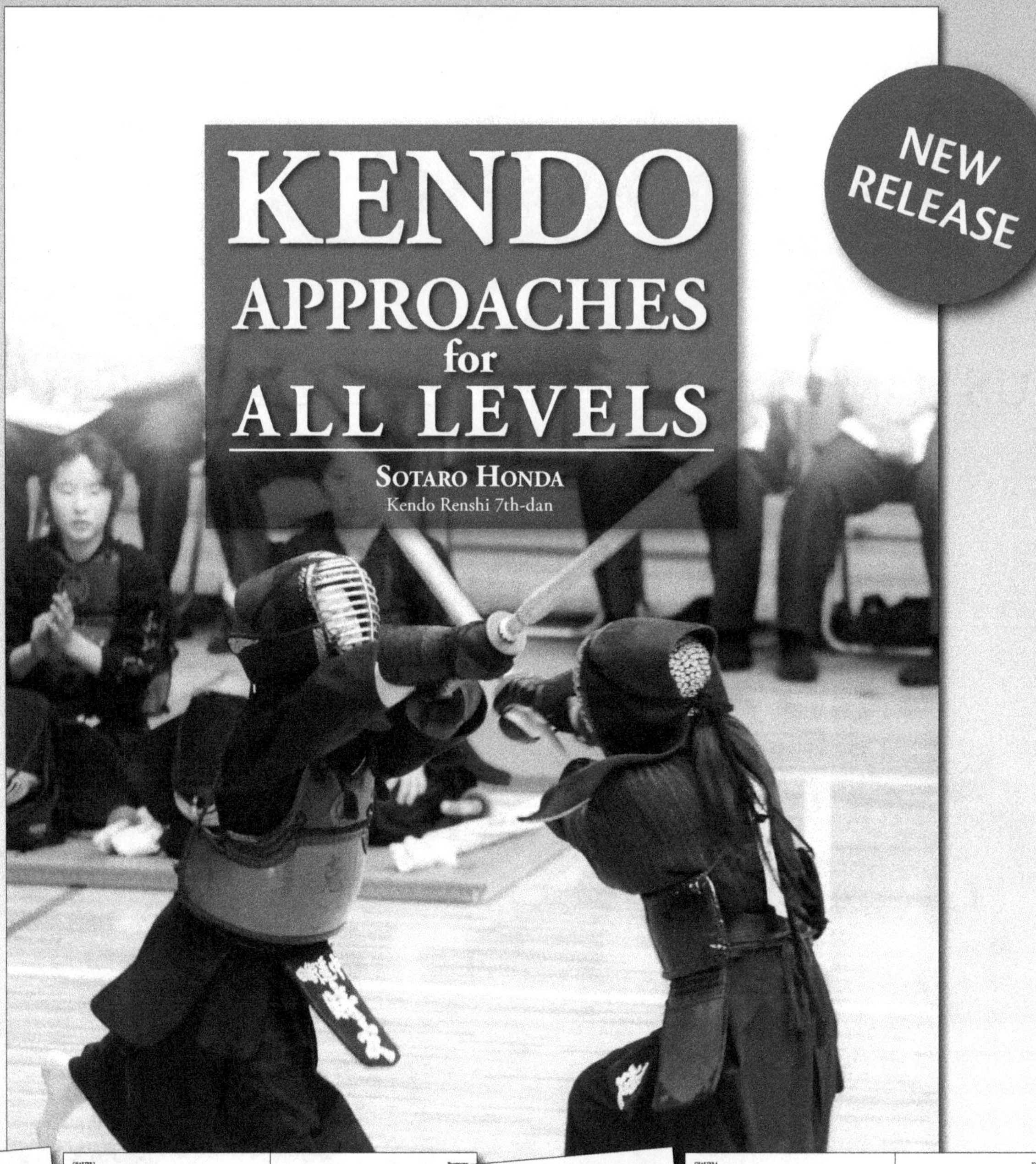

KENDO
APPROACHES for ALL LEVELS

Sotaro Honda
Kendo Renshi 7th-dan

NEW RELEASE

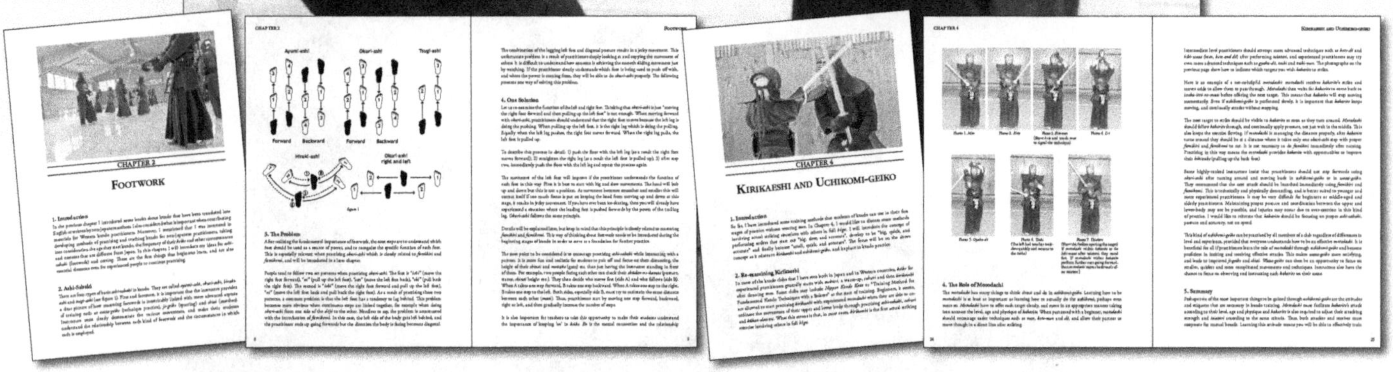

Kendo World is proud to announce our latest publication to enhance your understanding of kendo. Dr. Sotaro Honda (R7-dan), student of H8-dan Masatake Sumi-sensei, has been a longtime contributor to Kendo World, and has spent much of his kendo career helping international kenshi. His latest book is a must have for all practitioners and instructors, and explains various aspects of kendo training in a way that is both accessible and eye-opening. He covers the basics from footwork, to various *keiko* methods such as kakari-geiko and *ji-geiko*, and offers many useful hints for *shiai* strategy. Buy this book on Kindle as a download, or as a hard copy. See **www.kendo-world.com** for more details!

KENDO —Approaches For All Levels—

Sotaro Honda Kendo Renshi 7-dan   B5 size 102 pages B/W   **$25.00**

KENDO world
CROSSING SWORDS & BORDERS

KENDO WORLD Volume 6.3 December 2012 Contents

Editorial _____ 2

Hanshi Says **Kumamoto Sensei** _____ 4

Kendo and Asperger's: One Man's Story __ 7

Nuts'n Bolts of Kendo
Levels of Improvement and Keiko _____ 9

sWords of Wisdom **"Use all of your weapons"** __ 14

Thoughts on Miyamoto Musashi and the *Gorin-no-sho* _____ 17

An Interview with Hirata Fuhō Sensei
Musashi's DNA Lives on _____ 26

Bookmark **"The Five Rings"** _____ 29

Reidan Jichi **Kihon Dōsa—Part 3** _____ 31

Who was this Pioneer?
Takano Sasaburō _____ 34

Confucian Voices in Swordsmanship II:
Kenjutsu no Fushikihen _____ 35

Unlocking Japan Part 23: **Then and Now** _____ 40

Bookmark **The Truth of the Ancient Ways** __ 42

Shinai Sagas **Openings** _____ 43

A Bōgu Bag and a Duffle bag **Clash of the Titans** __ 48

Kendo that Cultivates People: Part 13
Grading Examinations _____ 49

The Kendo Coach: Sports Psychology in Kendo: Part 8
Aggression in Kendo—part 3 _____ 53

A Budo Camp on the Black Sea _____ 60

Fostering the 'Gut Instinct' _____ 61

Friendship through Crossing Swords _____ 64

Muslim Women and Kendo
A Look at How Kendo Has Been Embraced by Indonesian Women _____ 68

Bujutsu Jargon: Part 3 _____ 70

Bushido as Seen by an Englishman _____ 72

Kendo, Children and Competition _____ 74

Bookmark
Kendo—Approaches For All Levels— ___ 78

Hitler's Bōgu _____ 80

It's Academic
Notes From the Japanese Academy of Budo __ 82

The Development of Kendo in Slovenia __ 85

A Budo Camp on the Baltic Sea
The Dai Nippon Butokukai Naginatadō Kihon Dōsa _____ 90

Bōgu Revolution
The "Antimicrobial Bōgu for Comfortable and Hygienic Keiko! _____ 99

Kendo World Staff		Guest Writers
•Bunkasha International President & Editor-in-Chief— Alex Bennett		•Christopher Hellman
•Bunkasha International Vice President & Graphic Design— Shishikura 'Kan' Masashi		•Ivayla Ivanova (Kaiseikan Dojo secretary)
•Bunkasha International Director— Michael Komoto		•Kumamoto Tadashi (Kendo Hanshi 8-dan)
•Bunkasha International Director— Hamish Robison		•Nakano Yasoji (Now deceased. Kendo Hanshi 9-dan)
•Bunkasha International Director— Michael Ishimatsu-Prime		•Ōya Minoru (Prof. International Budo University; Kendo Kyōshi 7-dan)
•Bunkasha International General Manager— Baptiste Tavernier		•Peter Topić (President of the Kendo Federation of Slovenia)
•Senior Consultant— Yonemoto Masayuki		•Sumi Masatake (Kendo Hanshi 8-dan)

KW Staff Writers / Translators / Photographers / Graphic Designer / Sub-editors			KW would like to thank the following people and organisations for their valuable cooperation:
•Axel Pilgrim PhD	•Imafuji Masahiro MBA	•Stephen Nagy PhD	•All Japan Kendo Federation
•Baptiste Tavernier MA	•Jeff Broderick	•Steven Harwood MA	•Chiba Budo-gu
•Blake Bennett MA	•Kate Sylvester MA	•Stuart Gibson	•Hasegawa Teiichi - President, Hasegawa Corporation
•Bruce Flanagan MA	•Lockie Jackson PhD	•Taylor Winter	•*Kendo Jidai* Magazine
•Bryan Peterson	•Miho Maki	•Tony Cundy	•*Kendo Nihon* Magazine
•Charlie Kondek	•Paul Benson	•Trevor Jones	•Nippon Budokan Foundation
•Gabriel Weitzner	•Scott Huegel (MaSC)	•Tyler Rothmar	•TOZANDO
•Honda Sōtarō PhD	•Sergio Boffa PhD	•Vivian Yung	

COPYRIGHT 2012 Bunkasha International Corporation. No part of this publication may be reproduced in any form whatsoever without written permission from the publisher, except by writers who are permitted to quote brief passages for the purpose of review or reference. Kindly contact Bunkasha International Corporation at info@kendo-world.com.
Editorial Conventions Used in KW Inevitably in a magazine of this nature, many non-English words appear in the text. All Japanese words are italicised and include macrons (û, ô) etc., apart from common place names and nouns, and words in some captions and headings. As a general exception, KW treats common kendo jargon, and all of the modern martial arts (budo) such as kendo, iaido, jodo, ranks, and so on as Anglicised words without using macrons. Japanese names are written in accordance with the traditional Japanese manner of family name followed by given name. Traditional *ryūha* are written with capitals and therefore are not italicised. 'Kata' with a capital 'K' refers to the set of Nippon Kendo Kata, and *kata* refers to set forms in general. The masculine personal pronoun is used throughout the text in some articles in the interest of readability, and is in no way meant to slight the significant contributions made by female kendoka.

EDITORIAL By Michael Ishimatsu-Prime

What? Not Alex Bennett? Alex asked me to fulfil the responsibility of writing KW's editorial for this issue. It is almost the end of another year, and one that has been eventful for Kendo World. This year we made the decision to release the hardcopy version of KW via P.O.D. (print on demand); this being the second issue. Printed in a location nearer to where you live, it means faster delivery and savings to you on the cost of postage.

Another big event for us was the "1st Kendo World Tokyo Keiko-kai" held on Saturday, June 30 at the Nippon Budokan. More formal than our usual get-together in Kyoto in May, about fifty people from 16 different countries gathered for this two-hour training session. We were very lucky to have had eight 8-dan masters in attendance, and the first hour's training was led by H8-dan Inoue-sensei, author of the *Kata: Essence and Application* book. Following that, the remaining sensei lined up for *ji-geiko*. Inoue-sensei has already started preparing his program for the next event which promises to be even bigger and better. We hope to see you there!

On July 19, 2012, something occurred that sent shock waves through the kendo community, both in Japan and overseas. Shōdai Kenji, the 31-year-old Kanagawa police sergeant, 2008 All Japan Kendo Champion, 2009 and 2012 World Kendo Championship team champion, was arrested on a suspected violation of the law on child prostitution and pornography. It was revealed that when Shōdai saw a 16-year-old high school student who did kendo on a social networking site, he sent her an e-mail requesting they become friends. In the process he told her his name, job, and that he was a famous kendoka. He requested that she send him photographs of herself without her clothes, which she did. Shōdai did not deny these allegations.

When it was reported in the newspaper, I commented to my wife that I doubted the story would go any further because Shōdai is only a big fish in our small pond. However, she disagreed because it is a public interest story: Shōdai is a policeman. She was right as the story quickly made it onto the TV news that showed many clips of him in action in the AJKC. In the end, I was even having to field questions about him from my mother-in-law, as well as friends who know nothing of kendo.

Shōdai was released without charge on August 8. When he was arrested, an official from Kanagawa police said that Shōdai would be severely dealt with depending on the outcome of an investigation. However, presumably because he was not charged with a crime, Shōdai received a three-month suspension on August 31, but resigned on the same day.

The near silence on the KW forums about this matter was surprising, certainly when compared to the story of Kim Kyung-nam, the Korean Taishō at the 2003 WKC who was convicted of raping one of his students. This is possibly because Shōdai was known personally to more of us. Indeed, around 13 of my Facebook friends were his at one point, although that number that has since dropped off. Among the people I have spoken to, reactions to this story have been mixed. On the one hand, people have said, "Well, what do you expect? This is Japan!" This is a country where sexualised images of young girls are ever-present in the mainstream media. On the other hand, Shōdai has been condemned for his actions. I personally believe that this incident shows incredibly poor judgment, especially considering that he is a policeman. He not only gave his name, profession, and kendo history to the girl in question, he also asked her for photographs. Would you really want someone with such a lack of discretion carrying a firearm?

As Shōdai was one of their charges, representatives of the Kanagawa police kendo department have been to apologise to the AJKF. This is no doubt a major embarrassment to them, especially as he was a former champion and national team member. However, should this be an embarrassment for kendo? I do not think so. That is something that should only be felt by Shōdai.

The AJKF's "Concept of Kendo" states that *"Kendo is a way to discipline the human character through the application of the principles of the katana."* I have been to numerous seminars and competitions where we are also told that kendo and other budo "contribute to world peace". But does it? Does the fact that someone practises kendo mean that 'world peace' or the 'betterment of society' is their goal? Not necessarily. Are we good or moral people by virtue of studying kendo? Again, not necessarily, as this incident with Shōdai demonstrates. I personally know people that believe in, and promote the qualities that kendo is said to offer. But, I have also heard of and seen the behaviour of some who profess to uphold these values, but do not.

Ultimately one's deportment outside the dojo is a matter of personal choice. Kendo can be a means to many ends, and if it is regarded as a way to discipline one's character or contribute to world peace in some way, then it has the potential to do that. However, the same could be said for religion, art, literature or numerous other activities. When instances like the one involving Shōdai are committed by kendoka, we should not be shocked that a fellow practitioner could do something as distasteful as this. Disappointed? Yes. Angry even, but not shocked. Shōdai is merely a man who should have known better. He is now a man who was in a job doing what he loved, but who now is unlikely to be welcome in any dojo in Japan. It is a damn shame and a waste of talent, but he was the master of his own demise.

To finish on a lighter note, as I am putting the finishing touches to this editorial, the results of the 8-dan grading in Tokyo have been published. Wow! The famous kendo documentary that features Ishida Ken'ichi and Miyamoto Kai challenging for 8-dan, states that passing the grading is like passing through "… the narrowest eye of any needle in Japan." Well, it appears that the eye has become even narrower. On the first day, only four of 963 examinees passed; the second day, four from 888 – a combined pass rate of 0.43%, strict even by 8-dan standards. Congratulations to those sensei who passed, and also to Roberto Kishikawa of Brazil (residing in Hong Kong) who, despite not being awarded 8-dan, passed the first round of the examination – itself a remarkable achievement.

As always, Kendo World would like to receive reports of seminars and competitions that you have organised or attended, or other budo related matters. Please e-mail your submissions to editor@kendo-world.com. Thank you for your continued support, and we hope that you have a great 2013 both in and out of the dojo.

HANSHI SAYS

A series in which some of Japan's top Hanshi teachers give hints of what they are looking for in grading examinations based on wisdom accumulated through decades of training.

KUMAMOTO TADASHI (HANSHI 8-DAN)

Translated by Alex Bennett - *Kendo World* would like to thank Iizuka-sensei and *Kendo Jidai* Magazine for permission to translate and publish this article.

Kumamoto Tadashi-sensei was born in Hiroshima in 1937. He joined the Hiroshima Police Force in 1956 and served as their Chief Instructor for kendo, retiring from duty in 1998. Kumamoto-sensei has represented Hiroshima Prefecture at national tournaments and served as an officer of the All Japan Kendo Federation. He passed the 8-dan examination in 1987, and received the title of Hanshi in 1995.

"Decisions without proper observation are reckless…"

"Three years prior for 6-dan, five years for 7-dan, and ten years for 8-dan…"

Promotion examinations are occasions in which your kendo skills are assessed. For this reason, you need to prepare properly beforehand. Based on my experience, the amount of conscious preparation required increases with the level of the grade. For 6-dan, I started preparing three years prior, five years for 7-dan, and ten years for 8-dan. This involved creating a detailed plan of action for my training, and sticking to it.

When you have established your goals, your progress will be greatly abetted by finding a suitable instructor to guide you. There is an old saying, "It is better to wait three years to find a good teacher than start straight away without." This is sage advice indeed.

Everybody who engages in the study of kendo has their own beliefs. However, these beliefs should not lead to obstinacy. You must be prepared to accept advice with humility and obedience, and try to incorporate it into your training routine.

It is also important not to limit yourself to the local environment. It is beneficial to travel throughout the county and train with people you normally would not get a chance to, and compare yourself with them. This practice was referred to as *musha-shugyō* in the old days. You will be able to see how you match up with people of a similar age or grade, and this will provide the impetus to train harder, and also an understanding of what is required to meet your objectives for passing.

When I was in the police, Ōmori Hanshi, my teacher, made me go and train at other venues. I was able to fight many different people and styles of kendo, and I remain grateful for the things that I was able to learn through this interaction. I listened to, saw and experienced many things that made me stronger.

Before the war, Kaneko Kinji-sensei was a middle school teacher who developed teaching methods for kendo. In his kendo textbook, there is a section called "Be Obedient". Inside it says, "Listen well, observe closely, and perform properly." This is useful advice not only for kendo, but for all things. He also writes that we all have two ears, two eyes, and one mouth. We need two ears to listen attentively, two eyes to watch things carefully, and only one mouth because "there is no need to complain."

In this sense, it is important to take advice on board obediently, and be grateful for the privilege. This means not only listening to direct instruction, but also watching your seniors and teachers in action, observing how they conduct their training, and correcting yourself accordingly. Listening and watching is how you make other people's knowledge your own.

Ōmori-sensei used to say, "The tradition and transmission of kendo should not only be focussed on technique, but also knowledge and the spirit." He was an ardent and dedicated practitioner of kendo until he died at the age of 80. He taught me many things about kendo and life, and guided me in the right direction. Your instructor is of immeasurable consequence in the way that your own kendo evolves.

"Pressurise with your kensen, ki, and technique…"

The quickest way to improve in kendo is to train with higher ranked instructors, and try to absorb various things from them. Then, train with people of a similar age and level and polish the things you have learned. If you do not have an opportunity to train with people of the same level, and are in an environment where the other practitioners are generally lower than you, always ensure that you train with each opponent with urgency. That way, you will develop a sense of dignity (*kurai*) and your technical ability will improve. If you do not do this, your physical techniques and nonphysical presence will remain underdeveloped.

You may be in a region where there are few people of high rank who you can train with. Nevertheless, there are many examples of people overcoming this disadvantage through making the most of the opportunities they do get, and by having a positive, proactive attitude. Your outlook and manner is vitally important, especially when opportunities are few and far between.

When training with people who are weaker or lower in rank, never become arrogant or let your guard down. Approach training with them the same as you would with a high ranked instructor, with the same feeling of resolve. To improve in kendo in the physical and psychological sense requires an opponent. In other words, you act as a sharpening stone for your opponent, and they act as one for you in order to polish and refine your skills. Such an understanding of mutual

Hanshi Says

Kumamoto Tadashi (Hanshi 8-dan)

cooperation for each other's benefit will result in wonderful training opportunities because you can take advantage of the resources available to you. At the same time, do not forget the importance of self-reflection and devising strategies to improve.

In the actual grading, be sure to first observe your opponent carefully. Then, make your decision (choice of *waza*) and execute your attacks with commitment, followed by *zanshin*. The famous Meiji period statesman, Katsu Kaishū, said, "When doing something, do it with reticence"—i.e., observe your opponent carefully first. "When doing something, do it with audacity"—i.e., when you have made your decision, let go and attack with full force. "When doing something, unpreparedness is your greatest enemy"—i.e., regardless of the outcome of your attack, always be vigilant and alert. Although these precepts were meant as a guide for daily conduct, they fit perfectly with my idea of what is important in kendo—"Observation, Decision, *Zanshin*."

It also connects with the teaching "*seme-uchi*", or to assail then strike. In the process of pressurising your opponent (*seme*), first you apply pressure with the *kensen* of your *shinai*. Next *seme* with *ki*, and then *waza*. I think that many kendoka neglect to apply pressure with the *kensen* and their *ki*, and only assail their opponents with *waza*. This is quite a low level in my opinion. "Decision" (choosing a *waza* to execute) without "Observation" (attack and defence, reading the opponent), is reckless. I think this is the most important thing to keep in mind in kendo.

"Have you been diligent in your study of kata?"
I am happy that the *kata* component of examinations has become stricter these days. It goes without saying that high level instructors should study the Nippon Kendo Kata earnestly in the course of their daily training. Through the study of *kata*, the practitioner learns how to meet the opponent, then how to strike, and ultimately how to cut. This progress becomes evident in *shinai* kendo. It is odd that people are so inclined to neglect *kata*. I have always found it extremely beneficial in learning correct posture, *kamae*, grace in movement, and respiration (not breaking *ki*). You will never know how useful *kata* is until you study it for many years.

In my younger days, Ōmori-sensei took me to Tokyo, and we visited Mochida Moriji-sensei's house. He was on his veranda waving a ruler around. He was training on his own. It occurred to me that famous kendo experts do not just train in the dojo, but take every opportunity they can get when people are not looking. This is the kind of effort required to become great. It is also essential to maintain your own thoughts (philosophy) of kendo. To understand *jiri-itchi* (technique and principles as one) requires that one study books on kendo, including the old classics, to really access the philosophical backbone.

It will not do just to be great at kendo. It is obligatory for a kendoka to develop his or her character and be respected in the community, and to be able to make a contribution to society at large. Those in positions of instruction should never forget this.

The relationships I have had with great teachers and kendo friends are a huge asset in my life. I believe in the opinion of Ōmori-sensei, "Kendo is a magnificent cultural legacy which has been bequeathed to us by our forebears." As with the old saying, "Fill an old leather pouch with fresh water", we have been given an ancient vessel which can be constantly filled and used to quench the needs of people for ensuing generations. That is why I am dedicated to promoting and conveying correct kendo.

Kendo and Asperger's: One Man's Story

By Charlie Kondek
Photos by Alex Maynard

Ted Koehler is a 34-year-old kenshi with Asperger's Syndrome. Asperger's is a classification on the autism spectrum of neural development disorders. A person on the spectrum has difficulty processing sensory information, which can include sight, sound, smell, touch and taste, but also a sense of one's body, social and other senses. No two people with Asperger's Syndrome are exactly alike, so it is difficult to give a general description of the condition beyond saying that people with Asperger's can have difficulty with social skills and seem narrow in their range of interests. Instead of a broad description, we would like to tell you about Ted and his experiences in kendo.

Ted's biggest struggles with Asperger's are with social cues and, as he puts it, "fitting in with the group." Often in conversations he will hurry to get his words out, sometimes stopping himself to ask, "Am I monopolising the conversation?" He also has difficulty integrating loud sounds and touch. The cumulative effect of this pressure sometimes causes him to hesitate, and need to take a break from activity.

Ted lives and works on his own, and has his own car. He has had an interest in Japan and its culture for years, and studies the Japanese language. The last of his three visits to Japan, where he has friends, was for three months, during which time he studied at a Japanese language institute. This interest in Japanese culture is what led him to take up kendo at our club at Eastern Michigan University.

Ted does not have the dexterity or physical balance that neurotypical people have, so his progression in kendo has been a bit slower. In instructing him, we did not want him to get confused by too many details, so we taught him *kamae*, footwork and cutting in a briefer time span than we typically would. Also, we focus on the details while he is doing *mawari-geiko* with the rest of the club. The emphasis is, of course, on good *kamae* and cutting *men*, and Ted can now perform all the basic and combination *waza*.

Ted has been able to wear *bōgu*, but has had trouble receiving *men* strikes. Our solution for now has been for Ted to wear all the *bōgu* except the *men*. *Dō* strikes feel fine, and *kote* "stings a little", but *men* is very unpleasant, especially if struck hard. For the time being, Ted instead receives *men* strikes with his *shinai* during partnered practice. Recently, we have been working with him on receiving smaller, softer blows to *men* in order to build up his ability to receive *men* strikes. He rotates with the rest of the club and continues working in the beginner group, or performing *mitori-geiko* during the *ji-geiko* portion of practice.

That is probably the key to working with Ted: adjusting practice to allow him to address his limitations, and then constantly, gently helping him push them. Because Ted struggles with the physical activity of kendo more than a neurotypical person does, his body is often tense which affects his endurance. Consequently, Ted requires more frequent breaks; he takes them whenever he wants, stepping out of practice to catch his breath and get water, and then stepping back in when ready. We also allow Ted to progress at his own pace, not insisting that he reach certain milestones at certain times, but encouraging him simply to keep practising and enjoying himself.

Ted also requires a lot of encouragement. Anxiety affects him, and he will frequently become frustrated with himself. At those times, supportive words and a few minutes' break allow him to get back to practice. From time to time, Ted simply cannot attend regular practice due to feelings of stress, so we always let him know that we understand and will be happy to see him back at practice when he is able to. This extends to the 'second dojo', too – Ted finds having a milkshake with the club enjoyable, but does not usually linger over beers when the club gets together after practice.

Ted was hesitant about producing this article because he did not want to be seen as different, but he knew, too, that other people would appreciate or be encouraged by this information. The advice Ted would like to give to other people with Asperger's who are interested in kendo is to do it if you are interested in it. Do not give up when it gets difficult because you can do anything you put your mind to. To his peers, Ted would like to be seen the same as anyone else, and without labels. To instructors that might have students with Aspberger's, Ted advises what is expressed in this article: an awareness of the student's sensory issues, flexibility, encouragement and, of course, patience.

We believe this is just touching on the subject of Aspberger's and kendo, and would like to hear from other kenshi with these experiences, either as a student, a peer or an instructor of kenshi with Asperger's. Please be encouraged to share your thoughts with us either in the pages of this periodical, the forums at www.kendo-world.com, or by contacting us at charliekondek@yahoo.com. Ted's specific experience is with kendo as an adult, so we would like to encourage anyone instructing kids with Aspberger's to also share. *Gambare*!

THE NUTS 'N' BOLTS OF KENDO

By Nakano Yasoji, (Kendo Hanshi 9-dan)   Translated by Alex Bennett

LEVELS OF IMPROVEMENT AND KEIKO

Correct Kihon

How important is kihon?
From a technical perspective, the more bad habits you have, the slower your progress and improvement will be. As long as you take the time and make an effort to learn the fundamentals (*kihon*) properly, and use this base to build on and polish your techniques, you will gradually improve to a high level.

If you have a number of habits, you may be strong in some areas but weak in others, and this will hold you back. So, even though you might think of it as unnecessarily time consuming to keep doing *kihon* instead of working on more advanced techniques, stick with it. It is crucial that you are able to do *kihon* correctly and fortify your basic skills through arduous training so that you can learn to deal with any opponent. Improvement comes only after learning the basics properly and thoroughly.

Shin-jutsu, Ki-jutsu, Gi-jutsu

It is also said that you should start out with the basics. But, in fact you should never stop…
That's correct. I think that kendoka really need to pay more attention to working on the fundamentals. But what are the fundamentals? Chiba Shūsaku, the famous Edo period swordsman, taught the importance of *shin-ki-ryoku-itchi*, where mind, spirit and technique are integrated. Methods of the mind (*shin-jutsu*), the spirit (*ki-jutsu*) and technique (*gi-jutsu*) form the three supporting pillars of kendo. These are the most

fundamental aspects, and as long as you know this and realise their importance as the core of kendo, they will gradually come to life as you continue your training.

Each one of these pillars has a developmental stage. In the case of *shin-jutsu*, the root is the mind (*kokoro*). As you increase your training experience, you will be able to see things clearly, almost like becoming enlightened. Each time this happens, you take another step forward. As you progress and train at a higher level, you will eventually reach a state of no-mind or *mushin*.

Similarly with *ki*, you start by bracing yourself and emitting a fierce fighting spirit (*ki-wo-haru*). With continued training your spirit becomes more translucent (*sumu-ki*). The next stage of your development will see your *ki* will become vivid, but totally clear (*saeru-ki*). This is the highest level. With regards to *sumu-ki*, Miyamoto Musashi wrote that the spirit of combat is like the moon's reflection on the surface of a pond. With further forging through training, your confrontational fighting spirit gradually becomes less overt as it transforms into a settled, invisible, but intense *ki*.

As for *gi-jutsu* or techniques, the same process can be seen. At first you spend considerable time trying to master the basic physical movements. Although it is difficult to see at first, this eventually leads to the opening of the kendo "Way". *Jutsu* actually means "technique" or "method", but also means "plan". It is not enough to just keep repeating the same fundamental movements over and over. Although this is important, you must also work out how to use applied versions of the same technique. In other words, learning the techniques should be combined with planning on how to use them. This is how the techniques come alive. After much training, the practitioner will learn to access a higher spiritual realm of kendo through the medium of mastering techniques.

As I mentioned in the last interview, there are four elements to techniques. These are *maai* (interval), *hōkō* (direction), *kyo* and *jitsu* (falsehood and truth), and timing. All people alternate between the states of readiness (truth) and being unprepared (falsehood). Like the second hand on a clock, when it moves it is untouchable like being in a state of *jitsu*; but it will stop temporarily before moving again, and this is akin to a state of un-readiness (falsehood) which can be capitalised on. If you can identify this, *jitsu* will become *kyo*, and you will be able to strike your opponent without impediment. Another point for consideration is cadence or rhythm. Simply put, this is timing, and no matter how weak your opponent may be, he or she will be able to hit you if your timing is off. These four elements are entwined in the stages of progression for technical improvement, which as I have already mentioned, eventually leads to the Way of kendo.

The three pillars of the mind, spirit and technique are interwoven as one entity at the beginner stage through to the highest level. The master of kendo will attain a state of no-mind (*mushin*), with a powerful but totally transparent spirit (*saeru-ki*), and sublime technical skill which represents the absolute truth (*shinri*) of the Way (*michi*) in the search of knowledge. The ideal of *michi* encompasses a single objective from the outset. The practitioner trains to master the Way as if drawing an everlasting spiral. It is often a hard and arduous journey, but it leads the practitioner to higher plains of understanding.

The Various Levels

Please explain the process for improvement and what it entails.
There are various stages that must be passed through as one improves. At the most basic level in the path to improvement, is the stage referred to as "*shu*". This means to faithfully abide by the teachings that your instructor conveys; there are many variations of this. For example, it is said that you should start kendo because you enjoy it, and that way you will become better at it. There are many difficulties, and non-enjoyable

aspects that will be encountered; but if you stop when it gets hard, then it all amounts to nothing. To endure and pass through the difficulties requires self-discipline and a determination to overcome one's own deficiencies. It also requires the strength to endure and discard any self-pitying notions of hardship. To use a term from psychology, this stage requires "rationalisation".

Graciously, sprightly, correctly, and straight. Kendo should always be done in this manner. It should be performed with a big heart without transforming into a way for imparting suffering or vileness. This is referred to as "principled kendo", and it is a principled attitude that is required.

Also, one should retain latitude in one's training. There is no need to be in a hurry to succeed. It is important to maintain a bearing of normalcy at all times. Don't rush to triumph, but keep your composure and take your time, diligently participating in *keiko*. This attitude is necessary when embarking on the Way.

Next in the process of improvement is the phase of discovery and illumination. This is called the "*ha*" stage. Your perception of kendo will change here. When you suddenly realise something about your kendo that you have been doing wrong, you will take another step forward. Just going through the motions will not suffice. You should always be researching and seeking knowledge that will lead to a breakthrough in

your own perception. Each time you sense this is another significant piece of the puzzle put in place.

When you can evaluate your own kendo and make discoveries, it is an indication that you have gained a degree of confidence in what you are doing. A person who has confidence will develop a different expression on their face where a kind of strength is evident in the eyes. Your movement will become more vigorous, and even your nostrils will widen. This is a sign of self-assurance. You will also become more enthusiastic about doing things that you didn't like to do before. For example, you will start to enjoy participating in *shiai* more than when you didn't have the self-belief to perform well.

Miyamoto Musashi wrote that if a boat gets stuck in a fast current and you hurry to break free, you might capsize. Go with the flow and wait for the right opportunity is the message. This is the same in kendo. There are times when you will meet an impasse. Avoid becoming impatient and trying to force yourself through. To do so may backfire, and have negative effects on your growth. This idea is referred to in Musashi's teaching "Crossing the Expanse".

"The 'expanse' is crossed by piloting the boat, by researching the location of the 'expanse' if it is located on a sea route, by knowing the performance capabilities of the boat, by knowing well the favourable and the unfavourable points regarding the weather conditions, by making the necessary adjustments according to the conditions, regardless of whether another boat or boats will be accompanying your boat, by relying on a crosswind or by being pushed by a tail wind, and if the wind direction changes, by rowing for three or five miles, all with the intention of reaching the port…" (Miyamoto Musashi, trans. by Nihon Services Corporation, *The Book of Five Rings* [New York: Bantam Books, 1982], p. 64)

Another component is the "personalisation" of technique. This is the stage where you embody the *waza*, and they become your own. This initially involves constant repetition of the techniques to try and master them. This is unsophisticated and mechanical, but with practice, *waza* execution will become spontaneous, and you will be able to react instantaneously when provoked. This is an automatic reaction With even more practice, you learn to choose your opportunities for executing techniques. In this sense, the *waza* become selective and intentional.

The level above this sees your *waza* selection made subconsciously, again as an automatic reaction, but underpinned with an understanding of the higher principles. Your body and mind work in conjunction, and the right *waza* manifests at the right time. The mental processes involved in executing a *waza* comes naturally and without conscious thought but only after of years of training.

Finally, the "*ri*" stage indicates 'completion'. This is the ambit of no-mind. Musashi referred to it as the "Void". It is the supreme level where you no longer make conscious decisions. Instead, your movements and actions are all rational, natural reactions to the circumstances. Your *ki* or spirit also evolves here. As I have already mentioned, at first *ki* is rigid and forceful, like the sun pushing up from the horizon into the sky, forcing one's internal energy to the outside as fighting spirit. With practice, this spiritual force settles, and becomes sharper, and then finally transparent.

Thus, through these stages, the three pillars become one, and the practitioner becomes a true master of the art. Being cognisant of these pillars and stages in one's training is the fastest way to improve. There are many other details such as how to apply pressure on the opponent (*seme*) and so on, but this can only be understood through actual training.

Keiko Procedure

In keiko, there is kirikaeshi, kakari-geiko, ji-geiko and so on. What is the best way to benefit the most out of each training method?
I think that all of the various training methods are vital in one's development, but recently I have noticed that most people only train without being aware of what each type of *keiko* is for. It is important to make sure that regardless of what it is, it must be done with vigour and intent. In many cases, practitioners appear to be merely going through the motions, and this will not benefit their kendo in any way whatsoever.

If you are doing *kirikaeshi*, for example, do it with urgency. Then, after a short pause, refocus and do *kakari-geiko* with the same urgency. In other words, be sure to stop and think about what you need to do in each type of *keiko* first, without engaging aimlessly.

When doing *ji-geiko* against a sensei, the usual pattern is for both to hit each other a few times, then the trainee starts in *kakari-geiko* and finishes with *kirikaeshi*. I think this is a good way of training. It is important for young practitioners to be proactive and attack with as much energy and dynamism as they can. Attack with all of your heart in *ji-geiko*, then finish with a burst of *kakari-geiko* and then *kirikaeshi*. It is also important for instructors to ensure that students get plenty of time to practise *waza* as well. Otherwise they will not be able to develop their skills.

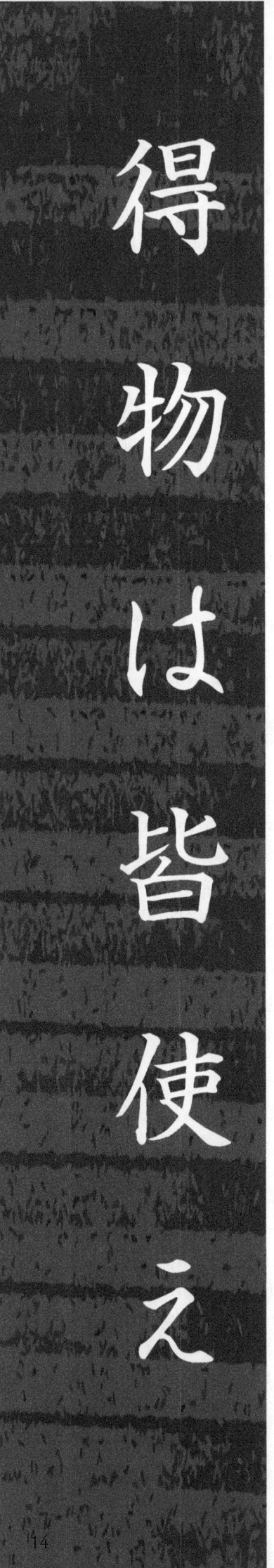

"Use all of your weapons"

Miyamoto Musashi (1584–1645)
founder of the Niten Ichi-ryū

"Warriors, both commanders and troopers, carry two swords at their belt. In olden times these were called the long sword and the sword; nowadays they are known as the sword and the companion sword. Let it suffice to say that in our land, whatever the reason, a warrior carries two swords at his belt. It is the Way of the warrior. Niten Ichi-ryū shows the advantages of using both swords."

Everybody who has heard of the great Japanese samurai, Miyamoto Musashi, also knows that he is famous for his style of using two swords at once, a style that is referred to in modern kendo circles as Nitō. Actually, he wasn't the first warrior in Japan, or the world for that matter, who cottoned on to the idea of using a short and long sword simultaneously. However, nowadays the two-sword tradition has become synonymous with Musashi.

There were a number of episodes throughout his life which influenced his penchant for bi-swordsmanship. Although many things surrounding the life and career of Musashi are shrouded in mystery or myth, and fact is hard to distinguish from fiction, the following events gleaned from various historical sources help us understand the evolution of Musashi's style:

1) When he was a child, he was enthralled by a priest at a local shrine who dexterously manipulated drumsticks in both hands.

2) When he was touring through the provinces, he passed through Bingo and became

SWORDS OF WISDOM

By
ALEX BENNETT
Based on the book
"KENSHI NO MEIGON"
by the late Tobe Shinjūrō (1998).
Used with author's permission.

embroiled in a peasant dispute over water. Holding a wooden sword in his right hand and an oar that he picked up in his right, he was able to block attacks with the oar and strike the assailants with the weapon in his right hand. This way, he was able to defend himself against multitudes of revolting peasants.

3) The weapon of choice in Miyamoto Musashi's family was the *jitte* of the Tōri-ryū. The *jitte* is a kind of truncheon usually made from metal, and is used for defending against sword attacks and bopping people unceremoniously on their noggins. However, it was not a common weapon to carry around on one's person. Warrior's generally carried a long sword and a short sword as a set, and Musashi must have realised at some stage that the short sword was similar in many ways to the *jitte*.

4) Musashi duelled with a warrior called Shishidō Bōin in the province of Iga in around 1607. Shishidō was renowned for his skill with the *kusarigama* (sickle and chain).

In the duel, Musashi, quite in awe of the weighted chain spinning over Shishidō's head, placed his *wakizashi* his right hand, *katana* in his left, and brandished his *wakizashi* in a circular motion to match the cadence of the whirling chain. Surprised by this, Shishidō started to retreat, at which point Musashi threw his *wakizashi*, pierced his chest, and then rushed in to cut him down.

Well, at least that's how the legend goes. This technique was preserved in Musashi's school, the Niten Ichi-ryū, as "*sanshin-tō*", or the "sword with three minds". One mind spins the *wakizashi* to get the opponent's attention, another mind is prepared to parry the enemy's attack with the *wakizashi* if needed, and the third mind seizes opportunities to jump in and kill with the *katana*. The act of throwing the *wakizashi* is also called "*hiryū-ken*" or the "flying dragon".

All these anecdotes make for interesting stories, but ultimately Musashi's motivations were driven by purely practical considerations. In the *Gorin-no-sho* he writes,

"Use all of your weapons"

SWORDS OF WISDOM

"If you hold a sword with both hands, it is difficult to wield it freely to left and right, so my method is to carry the sword in one hand… It is encumbering to hold a sword in both hands when you are on horseback, when running on uneven roads, on swampy ground, muddy rice fields, stony ground, or in a crowd of people… It is not difficult to wield a sword in one hand; the way to learn this is to train with two long swords, one in each hand. It will seem difficult at first, but everything is difficult at first." (Quoted from the Victor Harris translation.)

He does add a disclaimer by saying "When it is difficult to cut an enemy down with one hand, you must use both hands."

He saw the futility of being cut down when the resources at one's disposal were not fully employed. "When you sacrifice your life, you must make fullest use of your weaponry. It is false not to do so, and to die with a weapon yet undrawn." In other words, the underlying rationale for Musashi's style of swordsmanship was to make the most of your assets.

Even today as Nitō kendo that uses two *shinai* is becoming more accepted, especially among university students, there remains an undercurrent of cynicism towards the style. Some even think that Nitō is not entering into the true spirit of 'fair play' in kendo. But, all is fair in love and war, and Musashi's aptitude to identify advantages to defeat his opponents and stay alive gave him an aura that caused trepidation and served as a useful repellent against pesky would-be assassins. For example, Miyake Gunbei was a master of the Tōgun-ryū. He testified that he had two terrifying experiences in his lifetime: one was when he was confronted by frenzied enemies at the siege of Osaka Castle, and the other was when he met Miyamoto Musashi.

When Musashi appeared in Himeiji, Gunbei saw this as an opportunity to challenge the warrior to a duel, and hopefully make a name by beating the legend. Wondering what kind of man Musashi could be, he paid his lodging a visit and waited for him to appear. Musashi approached from the rear corridor with a *bokutō* in each hand. Even though he was meandering nonchalantly down the passageway, Gunbei felt a shiver go down his spine. He knew he was defeated before the duel even started.

Although there is much conjecture surrounding the true Musashi, one thing is for certain: he was a fearsome warrior whose pragmatism and versatility was his best weapon. The legend of Musashi has been immortalised.

Thoughts on Miyamoto Musashi & The *Gorin-no-sho*

By Michael Ishimatsu-Prime

There is arguably no more revered a samurai in Japan and beyond, than Shinmen Musashi-no-Kami Fujiwara no Genshin, better known as Miyamoto Musashi. He was undefeated in approximately 60 duels, and 2012 marks the 400th anniversary of the most famous—that against Sasaki Kojirō on the isle of Funashima.

However, Musashi was not just a swordsman. He appears to have been somewhat of a 'Renaissance Man', being an accomplished artist and calligrapher, and a practitioner of *sadō* (the Way of Tea) and Noh drama. It is a testament to his greatness that books, comics, Kabuki dramas and a plethora of TV programs and film adaptations of his life and achievements still continue to be made almost 360 years after his death.

In 1643, about two years before his death, Musashi climbed Mt. Iwato in the province of Higo, Kyushu. There, to purify himself, he bowed towards heaven, worshipped Kannon, and stood before the Buddha. In the Reigandō cave, he started to write *Gorin-no-sho*. Completed in the second month of 1645, this treatise on the "Way of strategy" would turn out to be Musashi's greatest legacy. *Gorin-no-sho* is still read by martial artists of many disciplines, is sometimes seen as a guide to daily living, and in the 1980s appeared to explain Japan's economic miracle.[1]

However, it is lucky that the *Gorin-no-sho* survived. A few days before his death, Musashi instructed his disciples to burn the manuscripts once they had memorised its teachings.[2] Instead, they made copies of it under the orders of the *daimyō* Hosokawa Mitsuhisa. We should be thankful to Musashi's disciples for defying their master's last wishes by not destroying the original text. Thanks to them,

---

1   To see the impact of *Gorin-no-sho* in discussions on Japan's economic growth in the 1980s, see Hurst III, G. Cameron, *Samurai on Wall Street: Miyamoto Musashi and the Search for Success*, UFSI Reports #44, 1982.
2   Tokitsu, Kenji, *Miyamoto Musashi: His Life and Writings*, Shambhala, Boston, 2004, trans. Sherab Chodzin Kohn, pp.246-7.

we are able to read and study *Gorin-no-sho* today, a martial art classic consisting of the five chapters of Earth, Water, Fire, Wind and Void.

地 —Earth

Explains what the martial arts are, and the essence of his school the Niten Ichi-ryū. Musashi asserts that the way of the martial arts should be put into practice by commanders, and that soldiers should know it well, but in reality there are no warriors who understand the way clearly, and few who actually relish it.

Musashi is famous for simultaneously using two swords, one in each hand. In this chapter he gives his reasons for why this is so. Samurai always carried two swords: the *katana*, the principle weapon usually wielded with two hands; and the *wakizashi*, the shorter sword that remained tucked in at the waist. However, Musashi wrote that in a matter of life and death, you should use both weapons. There is no use in dying with a weapon idly worn at the waist. According to Musashi, it is easier to wield a sword with one hand rather than two. While difficult to do so at first, it will become possible through repeated practice. By being able to freely use the *katana* and the *wakizashi* together, the warrior should be able to attain victory in any situation.

The way of the martial arts is likened by Musashi to the work of a carpenter. The master carpenter, who would be the commanding general, has to know which quality of wood is best for pillars, doors and lintels. Also he should know the merits and demerits of the carpenters that work for him, and assign them to specific jobs depending on their ability. According to Musashi, the principles of the martial arts are the same. It is important to take stock of what you have and what it can and cannot be used for. Being able to assess the situation in this way will help you in all walks of life, not just carpentry or the martial arts. As Musashi says, "The Way of Strategy is the real Way."

水 —Water

This chapter describes the fundamentals of combat. At the beginning of the chapter, Musashi states that it is important to deeply consider what is written in *Gorin-no-sho*, word-by-word, character-by-character. If the study of it is approached in a half-hearted manner, you will diverge from the Way. Musashi asserts that you should consider what is written to be just for you, and seek to internalise it—not imitate it—making it a part of your physical self.

Before any explanation of technique, there is a discussion of the correct frame of mind for the martial arts, which, according to Musashi, is more important than the body. The mind should be the same as the "everyday mind". It should be broad and straight, and neither tight nor slack—sway peacefully and never stop in one place. There is instruction on how to posture the body and position the neck, back, hips and feet. Again, as with the mind, the "everyday body" should be for the martial arts and vice versa.

There is also an explanation of the way to hold the sword, the use of the feet (always together, never one on its own), the five stances (upper, middle, lower, left, right), and that no matter what stance is used, it is important to not think of the stance itself. The only thought should be that of "cutting down the opponent."

There are numerous explanations of the techniques of the Niten Ichi-ryū for striking and parrying, and the circumstances in which they should be used. Many of the explanations end with, "Consider this deeply", "Research this thoroughly" and "Drill yourself carefully." The reader has been given the basics, but they still need to practice and face opponents to understand the underlying principles. This is like the maxim that is often found written on *tenugui*: 百錬自得 (*hyakuren-jitoku*—train well, realise by yourself). This is fairly symptomatic of a Japanese method of instruction—little instruction is often given, and students are usually left to work things out for themselves.

火 —Fire

Fire discusses the mental aspects of both individual and large scale combat, but begins with a criticism of other martial artists. Musashi contends that too much of their time is taken up with small details; how to give themselves more speed. He also criticises the use of implements like bamboo swords for training. The Niten Ichi-ryū is different in that the student puts their life on the line, and through combat, they are able to discern the principles of life and death. Moreover, through this type of training it is possible to learn the correct cutting angle, how to cut, and how to defeat an opponent. Then, when it is time to wear armour, the mind will not be concerned with small details, whether fighting five or ten men.

There is a discussion of the three types of initiative (*sen*): the initiative of attack (where you attack first); the initiative of waiting (where you give a weak appearance, wait for your opponent to attack and then attack at the moment his rhythm changes); and the body/body initiative (when both attack at the same time). According to Musashi, this is the most important thing in the martial arts. As with many of the other ideas written about in this chapter—such as how to unsettle, confuse or stifle your opponent, or create an opening—the initiative taken is dependent on the moment and the situation.

Fire finishes in much the same way as it began, with a criticism of other martial arts. Arts that expound lofty ideals corrupt the true Way, a point discussed in more detail in Wind.

風 —Wind

Wind compares the Niten Ichi-ryū with other styles, which Musashi has a clear disdain for. He also asks how it is possible for students of these schools to win when they are merely like a performance art or a commercial enterprise?

This chapter is divided into nine sections which cover, among other things, the use of long and short swords, speed, and use of the eyes in other styles. By focusing on too fine a point, the martial artist is limited and therefore doomed to be unsuccessful. If he is in a situation where he is unable to use his favoured sword or technique, what effect would this have on his mind?

The above point is illustrated when Musashi writes about footwork used in other styles, including floating, jumping, stamping and crow's feet. According to Musashi, these are all insufficient because they are only useful in a few situations. For example, with "leaping feet" there are not many reasons or opportunities to actually "leap". Therefore, the mind will become preoccupied with leaping. The use of the feet depends on the situation. It could be in a swamp, in the mountains or on a road. In the Niten Ichi-ryū, the feet are used as if walking normally and changes in relation to the opponent's rhythm, ability and manner.

What becomes clear from reading Wind, is that the Niten Ichi-ryū demands that the mind be flexible and ready to meet the challenges and conditions that arise in each individual situation. This is something other styles cannot accomplish because of their rigidity.

空 —Void

Void is the shortest and most esoteric of the five chapters. In Earth, Musashi wrote that the reason for writing Void was so that it is possible to enter the "Way of Truth". Emptiness is nothingness. Emptiness is knowing the existent, which means that the non-existent is also known. It is misguided to be in the world and look at things in the wrong way, being unable to differentiate one thing from another, and then think that this is emptiness. It is the mind of confusion.

In Earth, Musashi says that after attaining the principles, you leave them. This is because in the "Way of Strategy" there is a natural freedom. Through hard training you naturally develop strength.

You are also able to understand the rhythm of the moment that you are in, and are then able to strike naturally. These are all within the "Way of Emptiness".

In modern terms, the physical side of this would be akin to muscle-memory. An athlete would be thoroughly drilled in the techniques to the point at which they do not need to think about how to execute them. On the mental side, their response would be instinctual. In kendo, this is the aim—to react to your opponent's *waza* with one of your own, without having to think about it.

Essentially, the theme of Void is that warriors should take the "Way of Strategy" seriously and not be ignorant of their responsibilities. It is also important for *bushi* to seriously study and reflect on the Way of Strategy. They should not be lazy and should strive for a clear mind. This is true emptiness.

Musashi's Other Written Works

Gorin-no-sho might be the most famous and well read, but is not Musashi's only written work. *Heidōkyō* (1605) was the first, and was written when he was around 20 after he had fought in the battle at Sekigahara. Musashi had fought in several duels by this time, most notably against the adepts of the Yoshioka-ryū.

Heidōkyō contains 28 articles on themes similar to *Gorin-no-sho*. The first few articles are similar to those covered in Earth, for example how to use the eyes, hold the sword, posture the body, and move. There are also articles containing subjects like those found in Water and Fire on techniques and initiative. However, *Heidōkyō* is considerably less developed than *Gorin-no-sho*. That should be no surprise as Musashi was about 40 years younger and less experienced. However, it is believed that the techniques discussed in *Heidōkyō*, while in part borne out of Musashi's own experience in battle, were based on the teachings of his adoptive father, Miyamoto Munisai, who was himself a skilled warrior.[3]

Musashi's next treatise, *Heihō-kakitsuke*, was written in 1638 after he had taken part in the battle to suppress the Shimabara Uprising on the side of the Ogasawara forces. Its 14 articles are an extension of *Heidōkyō* and it provides explanations of the technical aspects of swordsmanship.[4]

In 1641, Musashi wrote the *Heihō-sanjūgokajō*. He was then living in Kumamoto as a guest of *daimyō* Hosokawa Tadatoshi, to whom he was teaching swordsmanship, and who was by all accounts a skilled swordsman himself. It was on Hosokawa's instruction that Musashi committed to paper for the first time the techniques of the Niten Ichi-ryū.

The content of *Heihō-sanjūgokajō* is similar to *Gorin-no-sho*. Some articles do not appear in *Gorin-no-sho* but the ones that do are generally more developed. Furthermore, the intended audience of *Heihō-sanjūgokajō* and *Gorin-no-sho* is different. The former was written specifically for Hosokawa which explains its brevity. Musashi said that he wrote succinctly, whereas *Gorin-no-sho* was written to transmit the essence of his school.[5]

Hosokawa died in April 1641, not long after receiving the *Heihō-sanjūgokajō*. In 1643, Musashi started to write *Gorin-no-sho*, which was completed in February 1645. At the beginning of the fifth month 1645, about two weeks before his death, Musashi wrote his last work: *Dokkodō*.

Dokkodō consists of 21 short maxims that start

---

3 See Uozomi Takashi, *Research of Miyamoto Musashi's Gorin no sho - From the Perspective of Japanese Intellectual History*, in Bennett, Alexander ed., *Budo Perspectives*, Kendo World Publications, Auckland, 2005, p.47, and Tokitsu, Kenji, ibid. p.198-199.

4 Uozomi Takashi, ibid. p.48.

5 Tominga Kengo, *Shijitsu Miyamoto Musashi*, Hyakusen shobo, Tokyo, 1969, p.131 found in Tokitsu, Kenji, op.cit. p.130.

with an instruction on not turning your back on the various ways of the world, and ends with plea to never depart from the Way of Strategy. The 19 other articles guide the reader, for the most part, on daily conduct.

Looking back over the life of Musashi, it is clear to see that each of his works represent a different period, with *Gorin-no-sho* as the climax. *Heidōkyō* was written early in his life, and *Heihō-kakitsuke* after participating in the last of his battles. Then he recorded an almost complete account of his martial art as a guest of Hosokawa Tadatoshi. Perhaps sensing that death was close, he penned the definitive account of the Niten Ichi-ryū in the *Gorin-no-sho*. His final act was to write the *Dokkodō*, which contains scant reference to the martial arts.

In spite of its conciseness, *Dokkodō* is a valuable reflection upon, and expression and distillation of a lifetime's experience. Tokitsu contends that because of their succinctness, these lessons would have meant more to those who had already received the teachings of the Niten Ichi-ryū.[6] Whether or not that is indeed the case, many of the teachings contained in *Dokkodō* are still as valid today as were they were over 360 years ago.

Gorin-no-sho: Its Place Among Other Classics of Samurai Literature

In the section on samurai history and culture at Japanese bookstores, Musashi's *Gorin-no-sho* is almost certain to be there. *Heihō Kadensho* (commonly known as "The Life-Giving Sword"), *Budō Shoshinshū* (The Beginner's Book of Bushido) and *Hagakure* are also likely to be on the surrounding shelves. This is certainly the case in the English language section of the big bookstores in Japan. It is possible for the aforementioned books to be divided into two groups, one containing *Gorin-no-sho* and

Heihō Kadensho; the other *Budō Shoshinshū* and *Hagakure*. To the latter group, *Bukyō Shōgaku* (The Primer of Martial Education) and *Shidō* (The Way of the Knight), both by Yamaga Sokō, could also be added. It is interesting to compare these books with *Gorin-no-sho*.

Yagyū Munenori of the Yagyū Shinkage-ryū—an official school of swordsmanship of the Tokugawa shogun—was a contemporary of Musashi. Yagyū was born a few years before Musashi in 1571, and died the year after him in 1646. In 1632 Yagyū wrote *Heihō Kadensho*. In its three chapters, this book details the many techniques of the Yagyū Shinkage-ryū and is heavily influenced by the Zen Buddhism of Takuan.

Both Musashi and Yagyū's formative years were spent during times of conflict. Samurai in that era would have trained hard in *kenjutsu* and other martial arts, and probably had the opportunity to use their skills in battle. However, when the country was finally unified by Tokugawa Ieyasu in 1603, Japan was technically at peace. The samurai had to justify their position at the top of the *shi-nō-kō-shō* (samurai-farmer-artisan-merchant) social strata which they created. They reinvented themselves as administrators and as paragons of moral virtue for the other classes. In order to accomplish this transformation, what was needed was a different type of samurai, and the literature to educate them.

In 1665, Yamaga Sokō wrote the *Bukyō Shōgaku*. In this short volume there is no mention of military matters: it focuses instead on the ideal comportment of a samurai. Its ten short articles advise samurai on how to speak and interact with others, how to dress appropriately, and how to eat and drink sensibly. In the same year, Yamaga Sokō also wrote *Shidō*, which, while covering the same themes as the *Bukyō Shōgaku*, is longer and more developed.

Budō Shoshinshū was written in 1716 by Daidōji Yūzan. This book resembles a school textbook, but one for young samurai. It gives them instruction on

---

6 Tokitsu, Kenji, op.cit. pp.217-218.

how to choose friends, serve their lord and many other notes on how to live a good and worthwhile life. The only mention of military matters is the entry that states that a samurai should study the martial arts seriously.

Also written in 1716 was Yamamoto Tsunetomo's *Hagakure*. This book is slightly different from the works of Yamaga Sokō and Daidōji Yūzan in that Yamamoto is clearly lamenting the degeneration of warriors into selfish weaklings with no sense of loyalty or duty.

It is interesting to see the difference between *Gorin-no-sho* and *Heihō Kadensho* on the one hand, and *Budō Shoshinshū*, *Hagakure*, *Bukyō Shōgaku* and *Shidō* on the other. The differences illustrate the era and conditions under which they were written. For the samurai of Musashi's time, there was a practical need to be proficient in the martial arts. However, once the Edo Period had become settled, this was not the case so much anymore.

Musashi was a product of his time—probably among the last of his breed—and that is reflected in the *Gorin-no-sho*. He was able to roam the country in a practice known as *musha-shugyō* (itinerant warrior training) testing himself against other martial artists. This practice came to be prohibited in the Edo period through fears that duels may upset the delicate balance of peace. Furthermore, Musashi actually had the occasion to use his skills in battle. If Musashi had been born 50 years later, it is unlikely that we would have heard of him. He would in all likelihood have been a very different type of samurai.

Why did Musashi Never Lose?

In *Gorin-no-sho*, Musashi wrote that he took part in around 60 duels and was "never unable to take the victory." What modern-day martial artists or athletes can boast the same record? There are very few boxers who finish their careers with a perfect record, and those that do are sometimes accused of avoiding certain others to preserve their zero-loss record. However, it appears that Musashi purposely sought out strong martial artists, but why did he never lose?

Near the beginning of Earth, Musashi wrote that after the age of 30, he thought back over his life, and realised that he had not won his duels because of martial skill. He certainly had natural talent, but asks if his success was due to the deficiencies of other martial art schools. Maybe it really was that simple. Musashi developed a martial art that was technically and mentally superior to all others. Furthermore, he also wrote in Fire that his "Way is the way of certain victory", and it was possible to fight alone against five or ten men and be victorious.

Musashi also employed the use of "mind games" in order to create weaknesses in his opponents. For example, when he fought Yoshioka Seijūrō, he used the tactic written about in Fire called *mukatsukasu*—"agitating your opponent". Musashi turned up late which irritated Seijūrō, making him unable to enter the fight in a calm state of mind. He lost. He then fought Denshichirō, Seijūrō's younger brother, again using the same ploy and won. Then the third time, when scheduled to fight Matashichirō, Seijūrō's son and new head of the Yoshioka family, a group of the Yoshioka disciples waited to ambush him. As they were probably expecting him to be late, he turned up early surprising them and he was able to kill Matashichirō and fend off the others. This is the teaching in *Gorin-no-sho* called *sankai-no-kokoro*—"change of the mountain and sea". It states that it is permissible to use the same tactic twice, but never three times.

In 1684, Hatta Kuroemon wrote an account of two duels Musashi had in the fief Owari, modern-day Nagoya, at the request of Tokugawa Yoshinao, of whom he was a guest. In the presence of Yoshinao, Musashi defeated two warriors from the fief without making a strike. He was able to control and dominate his opponents using his *ki*, pushing them back and around the dojo walls.[7]

Another account in the *Bukōden* mentions a duel that Musashi had in Higo at Hosokawa Tadatoshi's request, with Ujii Yashirō, an expert of the Yagyū Shinkage-ryū. It says that Musashi and Ujii duelled three times, with the former not making a single forceful strike. Musashi was just content with countering Ujii's attacks, which were unable to penetrate Musashi's defences. Hosokawa was greatly impressed and decided to try his hand against Musashi, but to no avail. From that moment, Hosokawa ceased practising the Yagyū Shinkage-ryū and started the Niten Ichi-ryū.[8] Although the duels in Owari and those against Ujii took place in his later life, it shows that Musashi was able to control his opponents through the use of *ki*.

Musashi did not just fight against fellow swordsmen: he also engaged in *ishu-jiai*—duels against adepts of different combat systems. He dueled against a monk of the Hōzōin-ryū, spear (*yari*) specialists in Nara, and against the staff expert, Musō Gonnosuke. However, perhaps the most famous of Musashi's duels was against Shishidō, a practitioner of the *kusarigama*—a sickle that has a long chain with a heavy weight attached to it on the end. The sickle is held in the left hand, and the chain spun around the head with the right. The weight is then launched at the opponent and is used to strike them, or wrap around their sword. An account by Yoshida Seiken states that when Shishidō started to spin the chain, Musashi took the *katana* in his left hand, and with his right hand started to gyrate the *wakizashi* overhead, matching the speed of the spinning *kusarigama*.

Apparently Shishidō was surprised and started to back up. Musashi then understood that he had the advantage, and threw his *wakizashi* at him, stabbing him in the chest. He then he rushed in for the *coup de grâce*.[9] If this account is even true, it demonstrates that Musashi was able to improvise or adjust to the situation. In Earth he criticises other arts for having a narrow focus. He wrote that the way of achieving victory is by taking the initiative.

Despite being only speculation, these few examples may shed some light on the reasons why Musashi never lost. What Musashi wrote in the *Gorin-no-sho* is reminiscent of an oft-quoted phrase in kendo: "*katte utsu*"—win and then strike. From accounts of Musashi's fights, and from the content of *Gorin-no-sho*, it seems that Musashi won his contests before the first strike was made, and in some cases did not even need to make one.

Musha-shugyō and Musashi

At the beginning of Earth, Musashi wrote that after defeating Arima Kihei of the Shintō-ryū at age 13, and then Tajima of Akiyama when he was 16, he went to Kyoto at around age 20 to duel with famous martial artists. He then travelled around the country, fighting in about 60 duels, winning them all. The last was against Sasaki Kojirō when he was about 29.

Many *bugeisha* (martial artists) would embark on a *musha-shugyō* at some stage in their life to gain combat experience and perfect their technique. They would usually travel alone, without the protection of their families or houses, and even had to steal or hunt for food.

Musha-shugyō is still important for modern day kendoka. In kendo, before a grading or important competition, kendoka will usually step up their training and visit other dojo (*de-geiko*). Training constantly in the same dojo is beneficial because

---

7 Okada Kazuo and Kato Hiroshi eds., *Miyamoto Musashi no subete*, Shin jinbutsu orai-sha, Tokyo, 1983, p.183 found in Tokitsu, Kenji, op.cit p.106-7.

8 de Lange, William (trans), *The Real Musashi - Origins of a Legend II: The Bukōden*, Floating World Editions, Inc., Warren, 2011, pp. 30-31.

9 Yoshida Seiken, *Nitō ryū wo kataru*, Kyozaisha, Tokyo, 1941, pp. 198-200 found in Tokitsu, Kenji, op.cit. pp. 63-65.

your sensei is able to guide you. The downside is that through only practising with the same people, you start to learn their idiosyncrasies and vice versa. This is not meant to imply that *keiko* then becomes easy and has no value, but visiting another dojo allows you to test your technique against unfamiliar kendoka and is a good gauge of your current level.

In the run-up to my 4-dan grading, I also embarked on a *musha-shugyō* of sorts. I increased my training to maybe six or seven times a week, sometimes even practising twice a day. With a job and other commitments, it is difficult to fit this much *keiko* in. It also helps to have a very understanding wife… However, it was important for me to do as much *de-geiko*, and train with as many different sensei and kendoka as possible.

I practised with junior high and high school students, university students and adults—each of whom presented their own set of challenges. I trained in Chiba, Kanagawa and Tokyo, and then in places further afield like Osaka, Kyoto and Gifu at different competitions and *keiko-kai*. Being exposed to these new situations and opponents was highly beneficial to my development as a kendoka. The experience gave me confidence in my abilities, and also showed me the things that needed to be improved, not just for the grading, but for my kendo in general.

The Relevance of *Gorin-no-sho* to Modern Kendo

Not long after starting kendo in Japan, in June 2003, I was asked if I had heard of a famous samurai called Miyamoto Musashi and his book, *Gorin-no-sho*. I had not heard of either, but was told that as I was a kendoka, I should read it. I bought it in the hope that I could learn more about kendo. However, upon reading it I found that I had no understanding of the concepts and ideas that Musashi discusses because I did not have the experience in kendo. Disappointed, I put *Gorin-no-sho* away somewhere in my apartment, and there it stayed.

When I reread it several years later, I found that I was able to make much more sense of its content, and was able to apply some of the wisdom to my kendo. Many of the items that are relevant to kendo can be found in Water. With regards the eyes, Musashi makes the distinction between two different gazes: *kan* (観—the eye of observation) and *ken* (見—the eye of seeing). Because *kan* is strong and *ken* is weak, Musashi writes that you should attempt to observe (*kan*). This would mean to "observe" your opponent's sword and not "see" it, or be distracted by it, and the same is true in kendo.

The ideal way in which to gaze upon an opponent is to "observe" them from head to toe with *enzan-no-metsuke* (遠山の目付—looking at a far mountain). If your eyes focus on your opponent's *kensen*, you are unable to see their feet, or other parts of their body, and therefore cannot see their intentions. For example, if you do not see their right foot moving forwards, or their left foot being brought in, you are likely to miss the fact that they are about to attack. By looking at the whole picture, it is possible to observe and know their intentions through their posture. Conversely, if you want to strike your opponent's *kote* and you glance at it, your opponent will be alerted to your intentions.

Jōnetsu Tairiku (A Continent of Passion), a Mainichi Broadcasting System documentary from 2009, was about Teramoto Shōji, the 2007 All Japan Kendo Champion and 2009 World Champion. In this documentary, small video cameras were attached to Teramoto's head to film his eye movements, together with cameras that were synchronously directed towards his opponent. The images captured by these cameras were analysed by a computer. The results of the analysis showed that when Teramoto made a strike, his eyes did not move—he was looking at the whole of his opponent. This means that Teramoto was observing his opponent while at the same time not giving away his intentions by looking at where he was planning to strike.

In Water, Musashi also talks about the correct way to hold a sword. The little and ring fingers should grip it tightly, the middle finger should be neither tight nor loose, and the thumb and index fingers should grip lightly. If the grip is too tight with all the fingers, this will make the arms stiff, then the shoulders, back, hips and then legs. If this happens, it will be very difficult to move. Musashi says that a hand that is fixed or immobile is a dead hand. Being unable to handle the sword correctly and with speed will result in loss.

Also discussed in Water is *men-wo-sasu*—"stabbing the face". This does not actually mean stabbing the opponent's face with your sword, but rather, with the *kensen*, pressure the opponent's face. If they step or move their head backwards, you have created an opening and a possibility for victory. I was told by my sensei that many years ago, it was usual that when contesting an informal *ippon-shōbu* during *ji-geiko*, just making your opponent flinch was enough for them to stop, lower their *shinai*, bow and say, "*Mairimashita*" (You beat me!), conceding defeat without being struck. This shows just how important it is to break down your opponent's *kamae* before striking.

Shūkō-no-mi ("body of the autumn monkey") is another important lesson that is discussed by Musashi in *Gorin-no-sho*. This type of monkey has short arms, and Musashi mentions this because, in a way, you should attempt to strike with this animal in mind. If you strike by mainly using your arms, the shape of your body will become bent like a shrimp. Your hips will be left behind and your body will become unstable. The ideal way to strike is by moving from the hips and striking with the whole body. It will make the strikes harder and more decisive and your body more stable. It will look like your arms are shorter, when in fact they are not.

Fire discusses the mental side of combat, and here, there is also advice that is applicable to modern-day kendo. For example, there is *makura-wo-osaeru* ("pressing down the pillow"). Rather than being controlled by your opponent, control them and move them around as you want. It is important to stifle your opponent's techniques or actions at the moment they are initiated.

An excellent example of this was in the second quarter-final the 60th All Japan Kendo Championships on November 3, 2012. This was between the diminutive, former two-time champion, Uchimura Ryōichi of the Tokyo Police force, and Asahina Kazuo, a former policeman in Kanagawa Prefecture who is now a high school teacher at Yamato Higashi High School. Asahina had a height advantage which he used to great effect in the previous rounds to dominate his opponents. From the outset, Uchimura smothered Asahina's techniques, "nipping them in the bud", not allowing then to be executed. By doing this, he was able to control the match, particularly in the opening stages.

Musashi writes about the importance of *zanshin* in *soko-wo-nuku* ("pierce the bottom"), also found in Fire. This is where you have to completely destroy your opponent's spirit to take the victory. While their technique may have been beaten and outwardly they look defeated, there may still be something left in their heart, so it is essential to be aware of this fact and completely destroy them down to the bottom of their heart. In Musashi's era, not being sure of this fact could have dire consequences. However, for kendoka, failing to show *zanshin* could lead to an *ippon* not being awarded, being taken away, or giving your opponent an opportunity to seize the victory.

These are examples of only a few entries in *Gorin-no-sho* that are relevant to modern-day kendoka. There is still a lot more that can be gained from this book. It might not pay immediate dividends, but it will give you plenty of food for thought, especially as your understanding of kendo increases.

An interview with HIRATA FUHŌ sensei: MUSASHI'S DNA lives on

Hirata Fuhō was born in Mimasaka City, Okayama Prefecture, in 1942. Those of you familiar with the history of Miyamoto Musashi will notice an interesting connection: Musashi's grandfather was Hirata Shōgen (Musashi's original name was Hirata Takezō); and Musashi is thought to have been born in Mimasaka. Could it be that Hirata-sensei is a direct descendant of the great Musashi? Well, the answer is in fact, yes. Hirata-sensei is the 17th generation head of the Hirata family, and as an 8-dan kendo master, he carries on the legacy of great swordsmen in the family.

Hirata-sensei joined the Keishichō (Tokyo Police) and studied under some of the greatest post-war kendo teachers. Retiring from the police in 2001, Hirata-sensei has dedicated himself to the study of traditional Japanese arts, martial and otherwise. Apart from holding the highest rank in kendo, he is also an adherent of the Ono-ha Ittō-ryū and the Jikishin Kage-ryū. Interestingly, he is not a student of Musashi's Niten Ichi-ryū, but after interviewing him recently in Kyoto, I found out that Musashi features highly in his outlook on budo and life in general.

Kendo World: When did you start kendo?
Hirata Fuhō: I have been studying kendo for almost sixty years now. I started not long after the GHQ imposed ban on the practice of the martial arts was lifted, and I was a year-5 elementary school student when I first picked up a *shinai*. Because of the Miyamoto Musashi legacy, the region where I was brought up and went to school was quite a hotbed for kendo. I continued practising though junior high school, and by the time I graduated from high school, I had attained the rank of 3-dan. This was considered to be a very difficult grade to take at high school level.

KW: Did you decide to join the police because of your skill in kendo?
HF: In a way, yes. I think that it was a decisive factor in where I was placed after joining the force, and as a result it made me more determined to excel in it. When I entered the Police Academy, I was the only one out of 250 cadets who held the grade of 3-dan. After graduating the Academy, I was first stationed at a police station in Ryōgoku [the sumo district of Tokyo]. The work was hard, eight hours a day with one 24-hour shift every three days, but I still managed to train in kendo. Because I was

young and was 3-dan, my superiors seemed to take a liking to me.

KW: *When did you enter the Kidōtai?*
HF: At the time there were five Riot Squad (Kidōtai) divisions in the Keishichō. At the end of 1963, each division created a special unit for budo training. These Budo Units were made up of 15 judo and 15 kendo practitioners who were to study their respective arts for a year. All of the inductees were well-known within the police because of their skills.

The following year in May, 1964, I was transferred to the No. 3 Kidōtai Budo Unit after spending only 11 months on the beat. I was fairly confident in my ability before this, but I was in for a real shock when I met my sempai in the Kidōtai. They were so strong that it really took me by surprise. Until this time, I had pretty much cruised through kendo without much difficulty, but it was different now. This was serious stuff, and the trainings were unbelievably rigorous. It was nothing but kendo, kendo, kendo every day. We would do 30 minutes to one hour of *kirikaeshi* without stopping, followed by *kakari-geiko*, and then *shidō-geiko* in which we were summarily put to the sword all over again. It was so gruelling that we would start seeing black and pass out.

It was particularly bad after a night of drinking alcohol. It was a *fait accompli* that we would be throwing up in our *men* the next day during the *kirikaeshi* and *kakari-geiko* sessions. The instructors would thrust us on our backsides, and knock us all over the floor, and even out of the dojo! It was hell.

But, as a descendent of Miyamoto Musashi, there was no way that I was NOT going to endure it. This was always at the back of my mind. Actually, ever since I was a child, my father would drum this into me: "You are a part of Miyamoto Musashi's bloodline. Don't forget it. Grow some balls!" It was these words that always helped me grind through tough situations throughout my life and career.

In any case, my time in the No.3 Kidōtai was as hard-hitting as it gets, but that is where I formulated my ideas on kendo. Kendo is a martial art that derives from life and death combat. Training with the Kidōtai was as close to this as you can get in modern kendo. Every day was a battle for survival. It enabled me to realise the severity of what we were doing, and where kendo came from.

After a year in the unit, I really started to understand what kendo was all about, and sometimes even managed to strike my sempai! From April, a new influx of trainees for the Budo Unit was decided. I hoped that I would be able to stay on as an assistant, but this was not to be. I will admit that I was bitterly disappointed at being transferred to another unit, but I used the opportunity to go to Nihon University night school classes and continue to study while I worked as a policeman.

KW: *Who were some of the kenshi that you admired in the Kidōtai?*
HF: I was able to train with incredible kendoka such as Nishiyama Yasuhiro, Taguchi Eiji, and Ōta Tadanori. They all became Keishichō Head Instructors, and their skill was formidable. They were a great inspiration to me, and I aspired to be like them.

Nishiyama-sensei passed away a few years ago, but he was famous for his kendo [he was 1965 All Japan Kendo Champion], his penchant for alcohol, and his amazing artistic ability. His paintings are sought after items now. He was also famous throughout the police, even when he was a cadet in the Police Academy. Every night before he went to bed, he would do 1000 *suburi* without fail after a day of bone-breaking boot camp. People still talk about it today. I remember just before he died on May 6, 2004, he said, "This is the end. I have no regrets." A truly great man.

KW: *How was your kendo life after the Kidōtai?*
HF: I spent the rest of my career working my way up the ladder in the police force, and continued to train as much as I could. Whenever there were any police tournaments, I would usually be entered as the captain of the department I was in, so there was a lot of pressure not to lose. I therefore trained a lot.

When I was the Chief of the Ōtsuka Police Department, I was able to practise at the famous Noma Dojo every morning between 7:00 and 8:00. Apart from ten days at the end of the year, Noma Dojo was open every day of the week, so I trained there each day, and after that would go to *keiko* at the police department as well. In total, I was able to train over 500 times in a single year.

I would also do the rounds at various police dojo and sometimes back at the Kidōtai. I always had a set of armour and *shinai* in the trunk of my car, and would pop in for a fence at a police station somewhere, or a community dojo whenever I had a spare moment. When I retired from the police, I had the rank of 7-dan.

KW: *So you passed the 8-dan examination after you retired?*
HF: Yes, that's right. It actually became an important goal for me after retirement. It kept my head in the game, and I stepped up my training even more. As you know, the pass rate for the 8-dan examination is very low, but if you are going to do something you might as well aim for the top. The harder the objective, the more determined you become. That's all I thought about. I left eight sets of armour in dojo throughout Tokyo, and trained every morning, and at night when I could. I would manage to get up to 14 training sessions a week.

I also trained conscientiously in the Ono-ha Ittō-ryū and the *hōjō kata* of the Jikishin Kage-ryū for quite a few years. I found that studying the classical styles of *kenjutsu* offered important insights into the techniques and philosophy of modern kendo. People often wonder why I don't study Niten Ichi-ryū. There is no reason in particular, it's just that I have never been in a place or a situation where I can learn it properly. Of course, I do read the classic texts written by Musashi, and believe these to be true treasures in understanding kendo. In that sense, I consider myself to be a student of Musashi.

So, all in all, I don't think many people were training more than me. Of eleven attempts, I was successful in passing the first round of the examination five times. This is usually a 10% pass rate so even that is very difficult to achieve. However, I never made it beyond the second section of the examination. So close, yet so far away.

Still, I was never going to give up, so I kept up the intensity of my training. Then on my twelfth attempt, at the age of 67, I was able to achieve my goal and pass. Actually, I was in the worst shape I had ever been in on this attempt. I had a foot injury through overtraining, and to top it off, I had a dreadful cold. My nose was blocked, I found it hard to breathe, and my build up to the big day was far from ideal. I guess it was the experience that I had gained from my previous eleven tries that pulled me through.

Now I realise after achieving this milestone that here is still so much more to learn. Once I reached the mountaintop that I thought 8-dan would be, I see so many more peaks to conquer in the distance. Kendo really is a deep and profound Way to follow. There is no end to it.

KW: *In summary, after all those years of dedicated training and study, what is kendo to you?*
HF: Kendo to me is my life, and it is a blooming flower of Japanese culture. By training with the *shinai* with as much solemnity as if it were a real sword, I believe that kendo can be used as a way to develop one's character and humanity. This means that through kendo, we can become better human beings. There is much symbolism in kendo, and even the official badge of the All Japan Kendo Federation is a reminder of the high ideals that we seek. The badge has the three colours of red blue and white. Red symbolises "wisdom", blue is "benevolence", and white is "courage". These are qualities that lead us to a higher level of humanity. I think that the ideal person embodies honesty, kindness, sincerity, courtesy, physical and mental strength, intelligence, assiduousness, and perseverance. To me, kendo is a Way to nurture these virtues. This is what I have learned.

KW: *Hirata-sensei, thank you very much.*

THE FIVE RINGS
MIYAMOTO MUSASHI'S ART OF STRATEGY

Book reviewed by Jeff Broderick
Watkins Publishing, London, Hardcover, 272 pp, US$24.95, £19.99

What's this, yet another translation of *The Book of Five Rings*? Just what the world needed, since at last count there were at least ten different editions on the market, some by people who don't speak Japanese, many by people who think Musashi was some kind of business visionary, most by people who don't study martial arts, and almost none by people who practice sword arts. There are even a couple of comic book versions for people who like to see unrelated pictures along with their text. This "New Illustrated Edition" is also full of pretty photographs to distract the reader from the printed word. Bah! I think I'll just stick with my old paperback version by Thomas Cleary, thankyouverymuch.

But hold on just a second, David Groff is not only a longtime resident of Japan: he is also a martial artist who has achieved a high rank in iaido as well as trained in a branch of Niten Ichi-ryū, the *koryū* sword style founded by Musashi himself. He has chosen from the outset to call his edition "The Five Rings." That "Book of" part always struck me as a bit superfluous, too… Well, maybe this one deserves a closer look.

It certainly is a lovely hardcover edition, with a silky, metallic-embossed cloth cover and thick paper stock. Nicely brushed *kanji* characters separate the sections, making for a pleasant overall layout. The many full colour pictures are clear, tasteful, and well selected to actually complement the text. A section discussing rhythm, for example, is followed by a landscape showing regular, wave-like rows of tea bushes; a passage called "Exchanging the Mountain and Sea" is followed by a beautiful two-page spread of Mt. Fuji reflected in still water. These plates break up the text and provide the reader a moment of contemplation. This is not, after all, a book meant to be devoured in a sitting, but rather a work that should be read slowly, pondered over, and then returned to again and again.

But here is the real question: Is Groff's version an improvement on previous translations of Musashi's 1645 classic? To answer this question comprehensively, I would need to be an expert on translation studies and have some familiarity with classical Japanese. Unfortunately neither is the case, and a full comparison is beyond the scope of this review. I did however choose a section of the book, and compared it across a number of editions. From Cleary (1993):

THE FIVE RINGS
MIYAMOTO MUSASHI'S ART OF STRATEGY

> *The idea of the crimson foliage hit is to knock the opponent's sword down and take the sword over. When an opponent is brandishing a sword before you, intending to strike, hit, or catch, you strike the opponent's sword strongly ... you then follow up closely on that, striking with the sword tip downward (kissakisagari) your opponent's sword will inevitably fall. If you cultivate this blow to perfection, it is easy to knock a sword down. It must be well practiced.*

From William Scott Wilson (2009):
> *The heart of the Autumn Leaf Strike is in striking down your opponent's sword, and picking it up yourself. When your opponent takes a stance in front of you and is intent on striking, hitting or parrying with his sword, strike his sword strongly ... In the same moment, without letting up for a second, if you will hit him again with the lowered point of your weapon, he will invariably drop his sword.*

From this edition by Groff (2012):
> *In "autumn-leaves" striking, you knock down the enemy's sword and take it away. When your opponent takes up a position in front of you and tries to strike, block or parry, if you strike his long sword ... then immediately strike it again with a feeling of knocking it away, continuing your strike until your own sword-tip points down, your opponent's sword will definitely fall. This strike, if you train well, will make it easy to knock your adversary's sword from his hand. You should practise this thoroughly.*

If you are reading Musashi to brush up on your business leadership skills, then one version is probably as good as the other. But the fact is that Musashi was writing a highly technical manual of swordsmanship for a specific audience of his own disciples; for the iaidoka or kendoka interested in what Musashi was actually talking about, small changes in diction can make a world of difference.

While I am not an expert in classical Japanese, I did compare the versions above with the original classical Japanese, alongside two separate modern Japanese translations, combined with my own understanding of the technique, having trained for a number of years in Niten Ichi-ryu.

I think Groff's translation is at least as good as the others, and probably better. Cleary makes a definite mistake in saying, "strike, hit, or catch." Wilson mistakenly interprets the passage to mean you are somehow going to pick up the opponent's fallen sword, and leaves out Musashi's advice to practise. Only Groff correctly translated "strike, block, or parry," and correctly understood "take [the sword] away," not in the sense of picking it up, but of taking it out of the equation. I want to state that I picked this example at random; other sections might be less faithful. Even so, I think it illustrates the difficulty of translating a technical sword manual without a practical knowledge of swordsmanship.

In addition to the possibility that Groff's version is more correct than other editions, it is also more thorough: it contains a well-written introduction, comprehensive endnotes, and translations of *Heihō-sanjūgokajō* (The Thirty-five Articles on Strategy) and *Dokkōdō* (The Path Walked Alone).

So don't make the mistake of thinking this book is "just another Musashi translation." Not only is it beautiful, highly readable, and well researched, it may be the most faithful English translation yet produced.

THE GREATER MEANING OF KENDO

REI
DAN
JI
CHI

REIDAN-JICHI PART 14

KIHON DŌSA PART 3

By Prof. Ōya Minoru (Kendo Kyōshi 7-dan)
International Budo University
Translated by Alex Bennett

Some sections of the text incorporate previous translations of Ōya-sensei's work by Steven Harwood

Kihon-dōsa, or basic movements, refers to *kamae*, footwork and manipulation of the *shinai*. In other words, it entails all of the principles behind the striking and thrusting movements for scoring *yūkō-datosu* (valid attacks) in kendo. This article will analyse the finer points of *suburi*.

Suburi

Suburi is an extremely important exercise to memorise the fundamental movements of the sword (*bokutō*, *shinai*) and body in unison. It is absolutely crucial at the beginner level, and requires dedicated practice. The main objectives for doing *suburi* are as follows:

To learn how to wield the sword and body in a cohesive fashion.
To learn correct blade trajectory to facilitate effective striking.
To learn *tenouchi*, or how to hold the *shinai* properly, and the use of the fingers and hands when striking.
To learn the fundamentals of striking and footwork.

1. Jōge-buri (Big vertical swings)

1. Lift the sword overhead in a large motion while stepping out with the right foot. (In order to loosen up the back and shoulders, it is possible to swing the sword right back so that the *kissaki* touches the backside.)
2. Swing the sword down to around knee height while snapping the left (back) foot up into position behind the right (*hikitsuke*).
3. Then, stepping back from the left (back) foot, lift the sword overhead again and swing the sword down while drawing the right (front) foot back just in front of the left (*hikitsuke*).
4. Depending on one's level, *jōge-buri* can be done moving backwards and forwards, or to the left and right at varying speeds.

[IMPORTANT POINTS]

1. Always maintain a correct, upright posture.
2. Use *suri-ashi* (sliding) footwork.
3. You should not change your grip, or loosen your hands and fingers, when swinging the sword.
4. Both hands should not deviate from the centreline of the body in the upswing or downswing. Power should be equal in both hands.
5. Footwork and movement of the sword should be synchronous. In particular, the leading foot should move as the sword is lifted overhead; the following foot on the downswing. The *hikitsuke* should be completed just as the downswing comes to a stop.
6. If the *hikitsuke* of the following foot is insufficient, your upright posture will collapse. Make sure that the *hikitsuke* is snappy and powerful.
7. Take care that the left hand is not too high when the downswing is completed. The grip of the left hand should be light but firm, squeezing slightly inwards and stopping just in front of the lower abdomen.

2. Naname-buri (Big diagonal swings)

The movement of the body and feet are the same as *jōge-buri*.

1. Lift the sword overhead in a large motion while stepping out with the right foot.
2. Swing the sword down at an angle of 45° from right to left to around knee height, while snapping the left (back) foot up into a position behind the right (*hikitsuke*).
3. Stepping back from the left (back) foot, lift the sword overhead along the same trajectory of the downswing in (2).
4. Then, swing the sword down on the opposite diagonal from the left while drawing the right (front) foot back just in front of the left (*hikitsuke*).
5. Stepping forward from the right foot, lift the sword overhead following the same angle of the downswing in (3), then swing the sword down on the opposite diagonal from the right while drawing the left foot up just behind the right.
6. Repeat this sequence.

7 Depending on one's level, *naname-buri* can be done moving backwards and forwards, or to the left and right at varying speeds.

[IMPORTANT POINTS]

1 Both hands should not deviate from the centreline of the body in the upswing and downswing, however, the right hand is used to guide the sword on the diagonal trajectory.
2 Even though the downswing is diagonal, the *kissaki* should stop in the centre upon completion. The upper body should not change direction, but remain facing straight ahead.
3 Turn the wrists sufficiently so that the cutting edge of the sword ends up facing down to the diagonal left or right.
4 When practising *naname-buri* with *hiraki-ashi*, do not move too far to the side, and remain cognisant of the position of the imaginary striking target.
5 Make sure that the sword trajectory is constant for both sides.

3. Kūkan-datotsu (Imaginary target strikes)

Kūkan-datotsu is an exercise in which the *shinai* is directed at an imaginary target like a real strike. It is the next step from the previous *jōge-buri* and *naname-buri* swings, and should be executed in full spirits with strong vocalisation and firm *tenouchi* to make a decisive strike. Strikes can be made going forwards, then retreating to *chūdan* to start again, or can be done moving backwards and forwards.

1 Lift the sword overhead in a large motion while stepping out with the right foot.
2 Swing the sword down to the target height (*men*, *kote*, *dō*, *tsuki*) while snapping the left (back) foot up in position behind the right (*hikitsuke*).
3 In the case of a strike to front, right, or left *men*, the right hand is extended out at shoulder height, and the left hand is positioned at the height of your solar plexus.
4 When striking *kote*, ensure that the sword is parallel to the floor.
5 When striking *dō*, the *kissaki* should end up in a slightly higher than the horizontal position, with the left hand at lower abdomen height.
6 When executing *tsuki* thrusts, turn both wrists inwards as the thrust is made. Both arms should be extended with the elbows straight. Make sure that the *hikitsuke* is sufficient after the thrust. Forward momentum is generated from your hips.

[IMPORTANT POINTS]

1 Footwork and sword movement should be synchronous. The upswing should start as the foot starts moving, and the downswing as the following foot moves. Completion of the *hikitsuke* movement should occur just as the strike is concluded. Repeat the process without stopping.
2 The *hikitsuke* should be snappy, and the *tenouchi* firm so that the strike is always made with unification of spirit, sword and body (*ki-ken-tai-itchi*).
3 Always maintain an upright, correct posture.
4 Try to focus the power of the strike in the *monouchi* section of the sword, and direct the trajectory of the blade with steady *tenouchi*.
5 Relax the upper body and remove superfluous power from the shoulders.
6 Make sure that the right arm does not become too taut at the end of the strike.
7 Execute each strike in full spirits with a powerful vocalisation of the target name.

* * *

One way to do *suburi* is to start by lifting the sword overhead without moving, then swinging the sword down as you move your body forwards (or back). This particular method is not wrong. However, in order to develop bodily cohesion and learn to use the sword with the feet and hands in sync, lift the sword up as you step forward and bring it down to the target as the following foot is snapped into position. The strike should be concluded with the body, sword and mind in unity. My next article will investigate the fundamentals for actually striking a target.

Who was this Pioneer?

By Alex Bennett

Takano Sasaburo (1862-1950)

Takano Sasaburō was one of the most prominent figures in the formulation of modern kendo in the early part of the twentieth century. He was born in 1862 in Chichibu, Saitama Prefecture, and died in 1950. Learning the Ono-ha Ittō-ryū style of *kenjutsu* from age 5, he moved to Tokyo in 1886 and became a disciple of the legendary Yamaoka Tesshū, studying Nakanishi-ha Ittō-ryū. He also entered the Keishichō and became a renowned and highly respected instructor to the police. In 1908, he was appointed as a teacher at the Tokyo Higher Normal School, the precursor to modern day Tsukuba University. In this capacity he wrote a classic textbook simply titled *Kendō*, which is still widely quoted today, and exerted a profound influence on the development of kendo in schools and universities. He was also on the committee that created what is now known as the Nippon Kendo Kata in 1912, and in 1913 was awarded the highest title of Hanshi in recognition of his service to kendo, and his superlative skill.

As an indication of the merciless training regimes of his time, Takano Sasaburō recalled a harrowing experience of the infamous *tachikiri* training sessions when he was in the police. The following quote is lengthy, but will give the reader a vivid image of the merciless world of kendo in its early days, and the kind of training some of the men who became to be considered the greatest and most influential kendo masters of the twentieth century had to endure.

> Once, Takahashi Kyūtarō, Kawasaki Zenzaburō and I did "day and night *tachikiri-geiko*" where we kept fencing without stopping throughout the night. For the policemen from the Keishichō who participated, those who lasted this gruelling exercise were selected to travel around the country to promote kendo. At that time, in addition to the three of us, ten prominent kenshi were chosen to practise without any break from 6pm through to 6am the next morning. The session took place at the Azumabashi Police Station in Tokyo, and 'assistants' who were willing came from various stations to beat us to a pulp.
>
> By midnight my senses were completely numbed. If we stood in the middle of the dojo in such a dazed state, the assistants would throw us down and hammer us. We would not pass the test if we did not hang on until the bitter end, but at around 2am it got so excruciating that I really felt like quitting. Still, there were four or five of us still standing. If we stood with our backs against the wall with our *shinai* upright, they would drag us out to the centre by force, and strike and thrust at us making it hard to carry on. The more we persevered the drowsier we became because of the incredible fatigue. We became as tottery as a carp in rough waters.
>
> Nevertheless, the human spirit is an amazing thing. A big chicken coop was situated beside the police station, and when the first cock started crowing, somehow we were re-energised. With the growing light of dawn we came to our senses again, and we sought out the individuals who were pounding us a short while ago and gave them a taste of their own medicine. In the end, the three of us managed to survive until the end.
>
> Nonetheless, training from 6:00pm until 6:00am was a truly miserable experience. We were able to eat three helpings of rice gruel throughout the twelve hours, and visited the washroom three times. My body did not return to normal for a whole week. Although I snored loudly, my head did not sleep at all. All I could see in my dreams for a week were images of fighting with a *shinai*. Although it is crude to mention, my pee was bright red for a week as well because of the blood in my urine. Those were the toughest days of training in my life.

Is it any wonder that he is remembered as one of the "Shōwa Kensei", or "sword saints" of the twentieth century?

---

[1] Takano Sasaburō, quoted from *Keishichō Budō Kyūjūnen-shi* (Ninety-year history of Keishichō budō), p. 419

Confucian Voices in Swordsmanship II
剣術不識篇 — *Kenjutsu no Fushikihen*
By Christopher Hellman

Modern kendo is a very different art from the swordsmanship of feudal Japan. It has evolved over the years subject to a number of different influences, and has changed quite considerably from the art of previous years. If we look at the schools of swordsmanship in the Edo period, it is possible to identify certain currents that were instrumental in these changes. Among these were the adoption of the *shinai*, the creation of *bōgu*, and the many years of relative peace that saw the samurai class move from being, in the main, warriors to administrators and bureaucrats. This was coupled with changes in the dominant schools of thought in the country that became popular as people's roles in society changed.

Although much has been made of the connection between Zen and the martial arts, the role of neo-Confucianism remains far less well known. Neo-Confucian ideology and philosophy played a large role in many areas of Tokugawa society, so it is not surprising that it affected the warrior class in a number of different ways. As well as its gradual positioning as one of the dominant educational and political modes of thought of the period, it permeated many of the disciplines and practices of the warrior class, including *bugei* – the martial arts.

Much is made (and rightly so) of the moral and social teachings of neo-Confucianism, yet at its heart, Confucianism is also a deeply personal philosophy that aims at individual perfection. It is not surprising that this ideal should prove amenable to practitioners of the martial arts, for whom the goal of perfection was also of paramount importance. Beyond this, there were other strands of the teachings which could be assimilated with relative ease by the warrior class. But for all this, how did these teachings relate to *bugei*? It is difficult to make generalisations, as each of the many *ryūha* through which the fighting arts were transmitted had its own characteristics. What applies to one might not apply to others; however, there were some documents written during the period when neo-Confucian ideas were at their most popular. This gives a fascinating look at ways they were applied to specific *ryūha*. In my previous article I introduced the *Jōseishi Kendan*, written by the swordsman and Confucian scholar Matsura Seizan.[1] In this article, I would like to provide, as a counter-point, another work deeply imbued with neo-Confucian ideology, *Kenjutsu no Fushikihen* by Kimura Kyuhō.

Little is known of Kyuhō (c.1704-1764) beyond the details presented in the forward to the work itself. He studied a style called Unchū-ryū under Hori Kindayū, who appears to have added sword skills to what had previously been a school of the

---
1 Hellman, Christopher, "Confucian Voices in Swordsmanship, The Jōseishi Kendan", *Kendo World Journal* (Vol. 5 No. 4, 2011), pp. 67-71

spear, and was named second headmaster of that style. Although it is no longer extant, this style was closely connected with the Yagyū Shinkage-ryū, and it seems that the sword component of the Unchū-ryū could have come from this school.

Kenjutsu no Fushikihen (Ignorance in Swordsmanship)

Published in 1768, *Kenjutsu no Fushikihen* was written as a conversation between a sword master and a visitor to the school. This invites comparison with the better known *Tengu Geijutsuron* which also uses the form of a conversation to explain the author's ideas about swordsmanship. In fact, it seems possible that Kyuhō's work was written as a response to the earlier work—not only does it include references to another work that was critical of *Tengu Geijutsuron*, but he also takes some of the points it raises and discusses them himself. In any case, it serves as a useful vehicle for discussing the art of swordsmanship: the visitor's questions and criticisms carry the thread of the argument, as the master explains about his teaching and his art in more detail.

Although it is, for the most part quite easy to follow, it is still a difficult text in some ways, and one which deserves a closer examination of its more difficult areas. Some sections are quite straightforward, even modern in their reasoning with a clear logical progression: "I don't teach paired *kata*," he writes, "they are not realistic." Others leave us a little unsure, as if we might have missed something important. The text is full of terms such as "principle" and "virtue", giving it a strong theoretical flavour, but the author maintains the practical value of his art. How can we reconcile these two apparently conflicting attitudes?

First, we must appreciate that the Unchū-ryū should not be described as a Confucian school of swordsmanship. If the art has any particular spiritual foundations, they lie deeper in the past. We should regard Kyuhō, first and foremost, as a *bugeisha*: when he states his credentials, it is as a student of the martial arts, not as a scholar. However, it is still a work deeply coloured by neo-Confucian ideas, and it is these which are used to explain and justify the teachings of the school.

Neo-Confucianism is no longer regarded as a living philosophy, so it is not surprising that its tenets are not well understood. Among its main ideas is the importance of the "principle of Heaven", an underlying principle that exists within everything. For Kyuhō, this included the martial arts, and he believed that those *bugei* that followed and embodied that principle were effective, and those that did not do so, were not.

This is a substantially different approach to that taken by Issai Chozan in the aforementioned *Tengu Geijutsuron*, in which he sought to explain swordsmanship through a Neo-Confucian lens, but without the sense of personal experience and authority that Kyuhō gives us.

For Kyuhō, the mind was of paramount importance. He uses such terms as "original mind",

"unobstructed mind" and "no mind"—these may remind us of Zen Buddhism, and indeed there is a connection between the two schools of thought, but there were also important differences, as the neo-Confucians were quick to point out. For Zen, the "original mind" is transcendent and non-discriminatory, whereas for the neo-Confucians, the power of discrimination was an important attribute of the principle of Heaven, which naturally discriminates between good and evil, and is thus manifested in the original mind.

Other typically Confucian concerns, such as the teaching of ethics, occur repeatedly throughout the work. As noted above, a belief in a natural principle that underlies all things means that, for example, physical arts embody the same principles that inform ethics. There should be no conflict between the two. This also allows a writer to work at quite an abstract level, even when describing the concrete aspects. Unfortunately, without experience in reading this kind of work, there is a tendency to take everything literally. A more informed reading allows us entry into this world through taking these theoretical concepts as they correlate to physical phenomena. This is a work that allows us to do this if we view it as explaining the mental and physical components of swordsmanship, rather than treating it as a theoretical work.

The Master's Teaching

Kyuhō's arguments are precipitated by the questions put to the "Master" (ostensibly Kyuhō's own teacher) by a visitor. These centre around the master's approach to teaching, and it soon becomes apparent that the developmental path involved in learning the art is fundamental to Kyuhō's conception of swordsmanship. He explains the importance of instilling the beginnings of an understanding of the neo-Confucian underlying principles from the early stages of training. Rejecting the use of *kata* as a training tool (except in the very early stages of training), he also rejects the idea of allowing the student to gradually realise the principles from training in a wide variety of specific techniques.

Instead, he advocates teaching the student to react spontaneously to attacks, gradually developing and expanding on this idea, leading the student into a fuller realisation of the one principle that underlies everything.

> "The practical techniques that have been extracted from the principle are shown by utilising the path of spontaneous response."[2]

The visitor remonstrates with him, saying that it is not only natural but right for an experienced teacher to put his own experience to work by making examples for his student; but the master demurs, saying these are bound to be flawed, as they are the result of a partial understanding of the teacher. The proof of his opinion is to be found in the fact that of the schools he has visited, all of which trained using pre-arranged patterns, none had developed a high level of skill. He explains that this is because the practice is at odds with the principle.

Although he was writing in the 1760s, this clearly suggests something that might have been a forerunner to kendo. By that time *bōgu* had already been introduced, and Kyuhō also makes specific mention of the *shinai*, as well as the spear and *naginata*, as training weapons. His mention of the spear is significant, as it seems to have been in spear schools that a kind of free practice first became established. Early records show the use of *bōgu*, suggesting the possibility that they were in use in spear schools before sword schools adopted them, and even into the present day, the use of free practice with the spear makes up a major part of the Owari Kan-ryū practice. This school uses the *kuda-yari*, a spear with a short metal tube through which the spear slides to give it greater speed and extension, and it was from the use of this same weapon that the Unchū-ryū developed.

The neo-Confucian flavour becomes stronger when he begins to explore the links between ethical behaviour and utility in combat. Although the necessity for moral and ethical teachings to

---

[2] Hellman, Christopher, The Samurai Mind, Tuttle, 2010, p. 103

accompany martial arts is self-evident, Kyuhō goes even further and states that it is a pre-requisite for the successful development of skill. This is an area that flies in the face of modern understanding, and Kyuhō's defence does not seem particularly strong. However, this theme is one that constantly reoccurs in the history of Japanese swordsmanship, and it would be foolish to dismiss it merely because it does not tally with our way of thinking. Kyuhō's visitor also seems doubtful, several times questioning whether the style of swordsmanship Kyuhō proposes is feasible at all. Is it not just some kind of spiritual training with no real utility, either for fighting or for achieving enlightenment?

The master concedes that, as far as self-development is concerned, swordsmanship is only a minor way, but he then goes on to explain that one can use any path as a spiritual path when you put the principle into practice—even religions will only give spiritual understanding when the practitioner has reached the 'Way' him or herself. If one has reached that level, then swordsmanship can actually be every bit as spiritual as meditation or studying religious works.

Ri—The Underlying Principle

Although he refrains from explaining in detail, there are enough references to suppose Kyuhō is referring to something other than behavioural issues when he criticises the fostering of aggression in the training of a swordsman. In a technical sense, the desire to win involves the student in the minutiae of technique—what do I do if he does this? How do I respond to this *kamae*? When do I attack? All of this suggests a gradual accretion of knowledge, finally resulting in mastery.

Kyuhō rejects this, explaining that this approach fills the mind with doubt and questioning, making it unable to respond freely to what is actually happening. It is impossible to cope with all the possibilities of combat by studying each of them in turn. What the student must do is study the principle, and once he has realised this, he will be able to apply it in any situation that occurs.

This connects directly to another point introduced early in the work—that you must understand the principle for yourself. Quoting Confucius, he states, "The inferior man seeks the Principle from others."[3] This is not to be taken too literally—Kyuhō repeatedly affirms the importance of good teaching—but as a reference to the necessity for the student to discover the principle for himself; it is something that cannot be passed on. This would seem to be a criticism of granting certificates of accomplishment and bestowing on students secret teachings as if receiving these will confer ability.

This aspect of the work reflects the teachings of *yōmeigaku*, the heterodox school of neo-Confucianism based on the teachings of Wang Yangming (Ō-Yōmei in Japanese). In contrast with *shushigaku*, the orthodox school which received governmental support throughout much of the Edo period, and emphasised the distillation and gradual realisation of the universal principle through the study of its many manifestations, *yōmeigaku* scholars believed the principle was already within us and only needed recognising. The comparison

---

3 ibid, p.125

with *kata* and Kyuhō's spontaneous approach is too close to ignore. Kyuhō's master explains there is nothing additional to learn (beyond the basics): there are no secrets.

At this point, it is worth returning to Zen. Indeed, Kyuhō himself makes direct references to Zen. However, despite analogous concepts, neo-Confucian scholars were typically quite critical of Zen (and Buddhism in general); Wang Yangming was himself quite familiar with Zen teachings, but rejected them on several points. Nowadays, popular cultural references to both Zen and Confucianism frequently obscure the complex nature of both disciplines, with Zen having assumed a mantle of 'cool', and being associated with space, simplicity, freedom and mystical knowledge, while Confucianism is taken to represent order, control and conservatism.

However, neo-Confucianism had within it a variety of currents, and was far more than simply an institutionalised form of societal control. Unfortunately, the habitual use of concepts that most Western readers are familiar with from their Zen context can cause confusion. Kyuhō's work is a perfect example of this, and until recently, virtually the only reference to it in English language works was a short extract in D.T. Suzuki's *Zen and Japanese Culture*, where it is given a decidedly Zen treatment.

To be sure, there are Zen references: these include "Swallowing the waters of the West River" which refers to intuitively grasping a teaching—something surely familiar, to some degree, to every student of martial arts; and the title of the work itself, which contains a reference to Bodhidharma's famous answer to the emperor of China when asked the meaning of Zen—"*Fushiki*"—it is unknowable (or, I do not know), a reference in the final lines of the dialogue. The preceding discussion, however, places this firmly in a neo-Confucian rather than a Zen context.

Conclusion

Kenjutsu no Fushikihen is a work that stands on the cusp of the development of the *bugei* into disciplines more suited to the relatively peaceful world of the Edo period. It reflects aspects of both worlds—a concern for the value of the art in combat and a realisation of the possibilities it contains as a vehicle for personal development. Perhaps it is unusual in that it explicitly connects the two and provides a key to understanding neo-Confucian principles in a practical context, helping us to realise their wider applications beyond the realm of theory. Although we cannot say how influential this particular work was, we can regard it as an interesting example of a school of thought whose influence is still strong in budo today.

It is particularly interesting to me as it gives some background to what have become accepted, but perhaps little understood, attitudes towards behaviour within the budo world. Indeed, this work can be seen as an explanation of how a fighting art can be a discipline of self-improvement with a wider application to other areas of life, and how such a broader philosophical approach can increase its effectiveness as a fighting art.

References

Bugei Ryūha Daijiten, Takayama Honten, 1978.

Kimura Kyuhō, "Kenjutsu no Fushikihen", in *Shinpen Bujutsu Sōsho*, Shinjinbutsu Ōraisha, 1995 (Original work written 1764).

Hellman, Christopher, *The Samurai Mind*, Tuttle, 2010.

————— "Confucian Voices in Swordsmanship, The Jōseishi Kendan", *Kendo World Journal* (Vol. 5 No. 4, 2011), pp. 67-71.

Osano, J., *Zusetsu Bujutsuten*, Shinkigensha, 2003.

Suzuki, D.T., *Zen in Japanese Culture*, Princeton University Press, 1959.

Tucker, John, "Quiet Sitting and Political Activism, The thought and practice of Satō Naotaka", in *Japanese Journal of Religious Studies* (Vol. 29 No. 1, 2002) pp.107-146.

————— "Japanese Confucian Philosophy", in *The Stanford Encyclopedia of Philosophy*, 2012 http://plato.stanford.edu/archives/sum2012/entries/japanese-confucian/ accessed on 9/11/12.<?>

LOCKIE JACKSON
UNLOCKING Japan
PART 23 Then and Now

Twenty-three years ago, I peered out the window of a JAL 747 and stole my first glimpse of Japan. As the plane descended into the late afternoon haze, my first impressions of the place I have come to call home materialised. If memory serves, the very first things that struck me from my aerial vantage point were the striking blue tiled roofs of the (by Australian standards at least) tiny houses below. I also vividly recall noticing several golf driving ranges scattered around the suburbs below me, although, at the time, I had absolutely no idea what they were. Once on the tarmac, I remember helmeted, white-gloved ground staff waving friendly welcomes in unison to the plane as we pushed up to the aerobridge. I've heard that memory can be deceiving, but I can recall these moments as if they happened yesterday. And in this issue of Unlocking Japan, I'd like to reflect on some of the ways in which living as a foreigner in Japan has changed over the past two decades.

First off, when I began living in Japan, being a *gaijin* seemed to be a much bigger deal than I suppose it is today. Back then, school children would wave, giggle and shout at you on the street. People who hardly knew you would invite you into the privacy of their own homes – such invitations are rarely extended among fellow Japanese. Back then, there was a genuine curiosity about things foreign and foreigners in general. Remember, this was the height of the 'bubble era', and having a foreign friend – a Westerner, especially – seemed to confer certain social weight. Having foreigners as friends suggested that one was a *kokusaijin* (an international person). Of course, this is not to suggest that we foreigners were merely commodified or objectified by our well-intended hosts. Many Japanese sincerely wanted us to experience what they perceived to be the 'real Japan', and if we were able to do this, we could not but help return to our homelands with positive impressions of the Land of the Rising Sun. International exchange and understanding indeed.

To my mind at least, today things are somewhat different. Non-Japanese unquestionably have a more visible presence in society. Most high school children, for example, will have been exposed to Assistant English Teachers through the government's JET programme. There are more of us here now, and we are increasingly taking on a greater range of roles in society.

The next big difference between the 'old days' and the present is related to the digital revolution. Two decades ago, I remember making infrequent reverse charge international phone calls to my parents in Australia from a special public phone booth that was able to connect international calls. I remember cramping around a friend's shortwave radio listening to a scratchy broadcast of a cricket match in Australia, and I also remember having to wait until the Monday morning's newspaper to get the football scores from the previous weekend's matches. English novels were prized and passed around fellow foreign co-workers, because English books were, on the whole, rather expensive.

By comparison, today, the internet has made living in Japan so incredibly easy. I can watch my football games live over the internet – on my smartphone while riding the train if I wish. I can consume any media I desire through my computer. International telephone calls have become much cheaper, and I can talk face to face with friends and relatives back home using Skype and the like. Because of the net, it sometimes feels like I'm not even living in a 'foreign country' at all.

Culinary options have also markedly increased since I first started living here. In addition to an growing range of foreign food importers, mainstream supermarkets now seem to stock many of the essentials that were so hard to get hold of years ago. When I feel I can tolerate the crowds, I shop at Costco; and I can tell you without a shadow of a lie that when I run out of Vegemite, I pick up a new jar from a store inside Kyoto Station while changing trains on my way to work. It's that simple. Those of you who have attended the Kyoto Taikai in recent years will no doubt be familiar with the Sanjo Starbucks franchise that sits prominently on arguably the most central and prestigious block of land in that historical and charming city. Ah yes, time are indeed a changing!

But 'progress' is a double-edged sword, and for all the convenience that it has brought to living as an ex-pat in Japan, there are several subtle charms that are slowly vanishing. For example, when I lived in Osaka, just before midnight, an elderly man in a white coat would push his *ramen* cart up the skinny lane on which our house stood. The sound of his flute drifting down the lane beaconed residents into the street for a late slurp of his tantalizing broth. I'm told he passed away, and if it's late night *ramen* that you're after these days, that you'd have to go to the new Seven Eleven convenience store that they've just slapped up around the corner. Convenience indeed. *Sentos* (public baths) too are another subtle pleasure that seem to be dwindling from everyday life in Japan. They still exist, of course, and yes, there has even been an increase in the number of so-called *suupaa sentō* (super *sentos*) in recent years. But authentic, mom 'n' pop *sentos* are slowly being turned into car parks. And more car parks we can do without. These are just two examples of the intricacies of life in Japan that are, unfortunately, being swept aside by 'progress'.

Lamenting these changes is not to suggest that living in Japan has become any less enjoyable over the years. Far from it. But doing so does serve as a useful reminder of the importance the things I definitely do like about living here, and not to take those things for granted. Now, as back when I first came here, Japan, with all its *clichéd* paradoxes, is a place that continues to fascinate and intrigue me. It's a place I will never bore of. And in that sense, the more things change, the more they tend to stay the same.

THE TRUTH OF THE ANCIENT WAYS:
A CRITICAL BIOGRAPHY OF THE SWORDSMAN YAMAOKA TESSHU

Anatoliy Anshin　　　　　　　Reviewed by Hamish Robison

The amount of material written in English about Yamaoka Tesshū is rather scant, hence my excitement when I heard that a new book about him was out. I had become a Tesshū fan some twenty years ago after reading John Stevens' *The Sword of No-Sword: Life of the Master Warrior Tesshū* (Shambhala, 1984), and also started training in Tesshū's Ittō Shōden Mutō-ryū nearly a year ago, so I was hoping for some substance to get my teeth into.

Anshin certainly didn't let me down, although personally I could have kept reading for a while longer. Maybe his PhD thesis on the same topic is my next stop, especially for some more detail on some of the primary sources that were referenced (in great detail, it must be said). The complete book comes in at 186 pages, out of which 67 are notes. You will find yourself flicking back and forth from the main text to the notes as I did, as they are rich with extra detail, or mentions of some of the issues with earlier authors' works on the subject.

As Tesshū himself tended to shun fame during his lifetime, there has been little research done on him in Japanese, let alone English. Much of it is a retelling of many myths about the man, or, in some cases, questionable 'authentic' stories that cropped up after his death and contributed to his fame thereafter.

Tesshū was an extraordinary man, but to fully understand him, you need to understand the age in which he lived, and the age which he longed to return to, that of the pre-Tokugawa period *bushi* way of swordsmanship. Anshin starts with a brief overview of *bushi* history, with a focus on the intangible *bushi* cultural heritage leading up to the Meiji period, and the political events that Tesshū would become embroiled in as the Bakufu came to a close and Japan's post-feudal era began. He pays particular attention to the development of warrior culture, especially the concept of *musha-shugyō*, which was one of the strongest threads running through Tesshū's life, and serves to explain many of the things that are to come in the rest of the book.

There are some interesting facts about the changes to the teaching methods of budo in general over the centuries in Japan. Also of great interest to me was the background to the development of many *koryū* that, although are now considered to be solid traditional *ryūha*, in the Tokugawa period were anything but – the "flowery training" that met such disdain from Tesshū.

Anshin's analysis of the blatant commercialisation of the Jikishin Kage-ryū could have come from a Harvard business school marketing case study, it was that concise and understandable. This section may make many in the traditional budo world a little uncomfortable, but it was an obvious outcome from the transition to a peaceful society for the traditional *ryūha*.

This really served as a refreshing new look at an area I had not given much detailed thought of up until now, and served to really place Tesshū's later development of Mutō-ryū, and his lifelong pursuit of *musha-shugyō* into very clear context. His reaction to the general move away from practical swordsmanship, and his subsequent search for the real swordsmanship, becomes very clear, and I am sure many readers who do some study of *iai* and *koryū* themselves will find many parallels to their own thoughts and experiences in this area. It's a very concise, readable look at the development of 'traditional' and modern budo that will have you thinking.

While this detail was fascinating to me, the close of the book looks at Tesshū's development (or revival) of Ittō-ryū, the Ittō Shōden Mutō-ryū, and this was the part I was looking forward to the most. Obviously there was nothing technical in this area, but an in-depth look at how he trained and subsequently developed his own, revisionist, take on the practices of Ittō-ryū was very interesting. At around the same time, I had a chance to see both Ittō-ryū and Mutō-ryū *kata* demonstrated together, and that made many things much clearer to me with the background from the book. The conclusion, and the book in general, left me with food for thought about the nature of promotion and growth of 'traditional' budo, not only in the Meiji period, but right now, too.

Anshin avoids the common pitfall of writing a non-critical look at Tesshū, but rather than serving to diminish the man, although he does try to dispel a couple of myths along the way, being honest about his humanity certainly does not diminish the man's stature.

Even for those who have little interest in Yamaoka Tesshū, the parts about the changes in *bushi* intangible culture and history alone make it well worth buying this book, and had me re-reading it shortly after I finished it for the first time. If you have even a passing interest in the history of *kenjutsu* in particular and kendo in general, this book should be on your bookshelf.

SHINAI SAGAS — OPENINGS
By Charlie Kondek

For a time it seemed no one was going to "second practice" regularly, and then it seemed everyone was going. This must have been something Honda-sensei instigated. That is one of the roles he plays at Mokkei Dojo. He is an explainer, a facilitator, a bridge between the towering silence of Ogawara-sensei and the rest of us. I don't remember when or how I became a frequent participant, but I do recall Honda-sensei's instruction: "*Dai-ni dōjō* is the second practice. Kendo *keiko* is the first practice. Usually, post-kendo requires going to the bar so often it is called '*dai-ni dōjō*,' 'second dojo.' *Keiko* continues there. You have a beer with the sensei and with your other club members, and you make friendship and continue to learn." Honda-sensei, making his rounds after practice, would apprehend any stragglers. "Steve, you come to *dai-ni dōjō*? Okay, just one beer. You come."

I'm trying to remember where I was in my skill level when I became a part of this; I think it must have been as an *ikkyū*. I'm born and bred as a kenshi at Mokkei, unlike some who started kendo elsewhere and then came to the dojo—Japanese, Japanese-American or otherwise. There must have been some point at which Honda-sensei and Ogawara-sensei recognised I was in for the long haul and made sure I knew the importance of this aspect of the culture. Or maybe they just invited everybody. As I said, I don't remember my first time or at what point I became a "regular". Now I see it only as long threads of memories woven into a continuous cord that stretches back into a dim, golden past.

I do recall those first feelings of eagerness and bafflement sitting at those crowded little tables elbow to elbow with the imposing figures of the club's *yūdansha*, the most imposing figure of all, Ogawara-sensei, at the head. Mokkei's regular spot was a tiny, almost nameless Japanese restaurant on a short street between a drug store that was always closed, and a shoe store that looked like it had been going out of business for decades. You'd think in a setting like that, tired and sore from

Shinai Sagas: OPENINGS

practice, hunched over bottles of Kirin being shared ceremoniously among short glasses, straining forward to hear the conversations in accented English and half-Japanese, that even Ogawara-sensei would finally look human. But he sat erect with the cold, polite dignity of a temple guardian, remote father to an unruly brood of hand-wringing monkeys. It took some getting used to.

I used to beat the hell out of myself as an *ikkyū*. I was still making my body do things it had never done before, behave in ways that were unnatural. A new kenshi at Mokkei has to first acquire proficiency in *kamae* and footwork, then spend a great deal of time on the *men* cut. Even after he starts wearing *bōgu* and participating in *ji-geiko* there is an emphasis on *men*, a big swing with good fundamentals, an *ai-uchi* attitude in which you do not care if you "live" or "die." This is the part that is unnatural to most of us, the part that keeps us attacking, over and over with the same basic attack, with an implement still foreign to our hands, and no thought to one's own defence. We are picked off repeatedly by faster kenshi with more control, and a greater variety of *waza*. Fighting against someone at that same beginner level, we pound against each other like a pair of hammers. Or, on a good day, like the waves in Hiroshige's woodblock blending together.

After practice I always felt like I'd run a long distance race in manic sprints. These days of course, the exertion is as much mental as physical, but back then I and other kenshi at my level were being forged. I was always grateful afterward to fall into a chair at the little Japanese restaurant and drink my fill.

As I look back on this aspect of kendo life I see many faces. What was it I said earlier about threads? Each face to me constitutes a thread in a braid of people that have passed through my life. In other words, I have known some of these people for almost fifteen years, and others I have known only a shorter time, maybe three years, before they moved away. Still others I knew for a time, then lost frequent contact, then resumed the relationship again because for whatever reason they moved back to this place where I have stayed. I see each of these faces before me, and imagine them as I knew them at the *dai-ni dōjō*. I remember small or great details about them, how they sat, how they drank and ate, what they shared of themselves or contributed to the conversations.

Besides Ogawara-sensei and Honda-sensei, there is Mr. Nakayama, who has three children who have been a part of the dojo for as long as I can remember, and who now, I suddenly realise, are of college age. The Nakayama kids would always scamper off to another table to pour over magazines and handheld video games with some of the other dojo children, some of whom were Japanese only staying a few years for their parents' jobs; others more permanent parts of the landscape.

Mr. Nakayama always sat with the "old boys" and liked to drink and chuckle. He was a willing accomplice to Honda-sensei when it came to lightening the mood, getting others to laugh, or reinforcing Honda-sensei's improbable anecdotes. I was always struck by how relaxed Mr. Nakayama was in his dress, unlike many of the other Japanese I have known, who take great pains with the neatness of their clothing. Part of me suspected Nakayama was not so much liked as tolerated by some of the other Japanese—though we non-Japanese liked him fine. I always wondered why his English was so bad since, unless I misheard him or he misspoke, he was born and raised in Seattle. I only saw his wife at tournaments or other special get-togethers and she also seemed very un-Japanese in how relaxed she was toward him, toward kendo, toward her children. She seemed, to me, one of the few Japanese mums not hovering over her kids. When she wanted them to move, she grabbed them by the sleeve and gave them a good natured shove.

There is Sands, a stockbroker type who always looks fit and tanned, and would seem natural in any athletic setting anywhere in the world. And Pawel, a heavy, shaggy Czech intellectual with whom one can easily discuss music, painting and politics. Pawel has done kendo in half a dozen countries as

he's bounced between academic and professional positions before settling in the States—where he is underemployed and likes it that way. Mallory Kim was an architecture student who moved to Atlanta. Tom Grace worked shifts as a paramedic for the county and was apt to disappear for weeks on end as his work demanded. I'm not sure what's become of him lately. We saw little of Breckenridge for a while when he had his second kid, but gradually he's been getting back in the swing of things. Ando practised with us for five years, went back to Japan for two, then somehow persuaded his company to relocate him to the States again, so he has recently returned to us.

All these faces and more were part of my education in kendo. It occurs to me my orientation to them shifted as my understanding grew. For example, Mr. Nakayama is not very good. I think perhaps he has had a long absence from kendo and took it up again for the sake of his children. I remember at first being intimidated by him—older, experienced, Japanese. I wonder when it was I began to be able to take his *kote*, or realised I was actually as fast as him, and could penetrate his *maai* and *waza*. I remember catching up in skill and surpassing Grace, whose frequent breaks from dojo life allowed me to overtake him. And I remember coming to a place of equality with Pawel and Sands.

There is also a university club that comes often from an hour away to practice at the first and second dojo. I have always felt competitive with these college-age guys. There is a lanky *sandan* named Nygaard—wait, no, he is *yondan* now—and Mazurski, the *nidan* that helps him run a club of spirited adult beginner *mudansha*. They, too, crowd the tables of our regular spot, attend the not infrequent banquets at the big Chinese restaurants or Korean BBQ places. We go there for bigger gatherings and special occasions—birthdays, farewell parties, visits of various sensei from Japan, Canada or other parts of the U.S., tournaments, gradings, seminars.

You probably know the patterns of talk that take

Shinai Sagas — Openings

place at gatherings like these. At times, everyone seated around the pushed-together tables is participating in the same conversation, often being led by two or three people. Although an evening might begin this way, it is usually not sustainable, even when those two or three orators try to involve everybody. "And what is your opinion, Hirota-san? And what do you think, Mr. Levin?" The pattern shifts to one in which several overlapping conversations take place, with clusters of two or three people branching off to hold their own discussions with the persons nearest.

As the drink is poured and consumed, as dishes of food are shared, the talks get louder, bolder and more enthusiastic. Often, we'll change conversation partners, moving to another seat or even occupying another nearby table, or drifting outside to talk and drink while someone, or several someones, smoke a cigarette. Sometimes we'll switch back again, and often all the talk will return, if only for a short while, to the involvement of everyone at the tables, especially if the sensei are making pronouncements on some topic.

I guess there are a dozen stories going on in the club at any given time, and those can be discerned if you are a careful listener at second dojo. It's true, too, what Honda-sensei said, that the *keiko* continues here. I'm always amazed at how much we can talk about kendo—indeed, it seems we talk of little else. Second dojo is a place where you can ask deeper questions, get careful explanations—sometimes they are forced on you!—or encouragement and direction.

I recall this past year when both I and Mr. Nakayama struggled with the *yondan* exam. Nakayama was jovial in the constant current of criticisms applied to him and me at second dojo by the various sensei and *yūdansha*. But to my surprise I could see in first dojo how frustrated he was. His face beneath the *men* would grimace and wince as we'd clash, as when, say, I'd launch a furious, straight *men* cut at him and slam into him with *taiatari*. I could see in those moments when we strained against each other in *tsubazeriai*, that he cursed his sloppy body for not being able to do what he wanted it to do, for not being able to move as quickly as it had when he'd been an adolescent, and for not being able to keep up with his kids. I thought I could see in his face, uncovered when he removed his *men* at practice's end, deeper degrees of exhaustion because he was pushing himself so hard to attempt another try at the *yondan* exam.

My knowledge of the Japanese language is slim, but at second dojo on the occasions when he'd failed this *shinsa*, Ogawara-sensei had stern words for him that Honda-sensei did little to soften. Once, I thought I heard Ogawara-sensei say something like, "If you'd do what I tell you instead of smiling like an idiot all the time, you'd pass that damn grade." Nakayama smiled his eager smile but now I could see how he propped up that smile with his humiliation and pain. The day we passed "that damn grade" he poured a beer over my head and I embraced him like a brother. He seemed, on that occasion, to sink into his chair depleted, and had little to say for once, no jokes to make. In time he has gotten back to his old self, loudly embarrassing anyone within reach. His kendo has changed remarkably, too; there is something cleaner about it. I take his *men* just as often, but he displays more control and the *waza* he executes have more power, even if they are fewer than mine.

Fifteen years, almost. So now I am one of the old guys giving advice, demonstrating *maai* with a pair of chopsticks, pushing chairs out of the way to show footwork. And it occurs to me now that I have spent a lot of time with these people because of kendo. I realise that they are friends, good friends, but that I have always kept them compartmentalized from my non-kendo friends. Not, as I think of it now, for any particular reason, but because I just never got around to synchronising them with the rest of my life. I think the reasons for this are simply time and circumstance. Time: I have none, am already stealing it from other things to use it on my weekly visits to first and second dojo. Circumstance: I am not at a place in my life to pursue friendships as freely as I once did.

Maybe 15 years ago, when I first started kendo,

and then when I was newly married… But now? I have a lot of responsibility in my career, at home with the family. By the time I realised that I would spend more time with some of these people outside of first and second dojo, like to go to a movie with Breckenridge, or watch football with Grace, or go to some jazz clubs with Pawel and Ando, it was too late. I realised, too, that I was already giving to them as much as I could give, taking what I could take. It's a feeling like missing a bus, and not even realising you might have wanted to be on it until it leaves the curb and roars up the street. I look with mild envy on the friendships formed among the college age guys at Nygaard's club, how they seem to do much more together. But they are at an age and a place in life where they can.

And perhaps, too, a lesson is revealed to me here. Fifteen years ago when I first set out on this path I did not expect them to be more to me than the people with whom I shared this hobby. I assumed they would occupy the same degree of attention as, say, some of the people at work, or a friendly face in church. Yet even now as I write, it occurs to me to ask how much I know these people. But maybe that's the wrong question. It isn't a matter of how much I know, but what I know, and the way it is revealed. Like my glimpses into Nakayama's mortality and pride. Or the fact that I have penetrated Ogawara-sensei not at all.

I remember when my mother died, none of my kendo friends came to her funeral. None even sent cards. Not because they didn't care, but because they didn't know. I simply hadn't told anyone at the dojo, not for any reason except that it hadn't come up. Sometime after this, I happened to find myself at *dai-ni dōjō* with a smaller crowd than usual. I was at a table with only Breckenridge and Pawel. Somehow, as we found the bottom of our beers, the topic of kendo was for the moment exhausted and the topic of our lives came up. I mentioned my mother's passing and received the appropriate sympathy. And, for whatever reason, I tried to put into words something I had been thinking but never spoken. I said that when a man dies it seems to me he leaves behind strength, but that when a woman dies, light, colour and warmth go out of the world.

I still don't know what I meant by that—I suppose I mean that a father leaves a legacy to be taken up by his son but that a mother's love cannot be replaced in a son's heart. Anyway, it seemed to me something I believed, but which could have sounded silly spoken aloud. I don't think I could have said it in front of Ogawara-sensei or Honda-sensei, even if I thought it could have been translated accurately. I'm not sure I could have said it with as much confidence in any other setting; though I have tried the line a time or two since then, it never sounded as correct. But my friends seemed to understand me.

Ever since I became a *yondan* I've lined up on the instructor side for *seiretsu*. From there, I have an entirely different view; I see the club spread before me, from the most experienced *sandan* to the newest *mudansha*. At the end of a hard *keiko* this is mostly a line of blue-hooded titanium masks sitting in *seiza* with gauntleted fists reposed on kneeling thighs. At the command *men-wo-tore*, the helmet is removed, and I can see beneath each silvered cage a face of flesh. My eye sweeps the line a range of expressions: exhausted, satisfied, beaten, bewildered, triumphant, poised, panting, thoughtful, terrified, eager, concealed, and who knows what else. Each face is another chapter in an on-going story. I know as I gaze at them that I will be seeing them in an hour's time in an entirely new setting, perhaps relaxed behind a table beneath a poster advertising Sapporo, or bent over a pair of chopsticks picking at a plate of *gyōza* dumplings.

Kendo affords us the opportunity to express ourselves in contrast to others, to probe another's defences for *suki*, and attempt to capitalise on those openings with an attack. If successful, we make a connection, *ippon* is acknowledged, an experience is exchanged. As we attain higher levels, our instructors tell us our *keiko* must become a kind of communication as opposed to a continuous series of attacks regardless of *suki*. I can see now how much I've learned to communicate, and how much more I have to learn. I have begun to see the openings even if I can't always capitalise on them.

A DUFFLE BAG & A BOGU BAG

By Imafuji Masahiro

PART 9: CLASH OF THE TITANS

I started kendo at the age of seven in my home town of Itami City, Hyōgo Prefecture. That was in 1980 at Shūbukan, a dojo with a long history. It was established in 1786 as a private dojo called Yōbukai, which then opened to the public in 1869 and changed its name to Shūbukan in 1885.

A Scary Looking Old Man

Because there were so many children who wanted to do kendo in the early 80s, Shūbukan had an application day twice a year, and prospective students had to be over seven years old. When I enrolled in Shūbukan there were about 40 new students. Can you imagine 40 new students, twice a year? That was just for the beginner's class, and after graduation, there were over 60 senior students aged between eight and 12 years old.

There were at least four instructors teaching the novice classes. They also taught the advanced students. One old man beating a *taiko* was giving commands. He seemed tall for someone his age, and he was the scariest looking sensei there. He was ordering around the other *sensei*, who were themselves pretty scary! He was the late Tsurumaru Juichi-senei, an 8-dan when I started, but who became a 9-dan in May 1992. Of course, I did not know how good he was, and neither did my parents. He was just a frightening old grandpa!

Basics, Basics, Basics!

I think it took us about six months until we could put on *bōgu*. Beginners were not allowed to wear *men* straight away, so we practised with only *tare*, *dō* and *kote* until we got used to it. When we had learned *tandoku-dōsa* (one-person training) we started *sōtai-dōsa* (pair work). We practised basic strikes to *men*, *kote* and *dō* as well as *kirikaeshi*. Finally we were able to put our *men* on, and in addition to basic striking and *kirikaeshi*, we also learned *uchikomi*.

We had a one-hour class three times a week. Twice a week we did nothing but *kirikaeshi* and *uchikomi*, and only had *ji-geiko* on one day. There were at least 60 students in the dojo so we all had to take our turn, and could only do about ten bouts of *ji-geiko* per week, or less. This did not change until we graduated from primary school at 12 years of age. Tsurumaru-sensei did not allow anyone who could not perform *kirikaeshi* satisfactorily to join in with *ji-geiko* and *uchikomi*. The basics were everything, and he was particularly strict with *kirikaeshi*. We never learned any techniques in five years of training.

The Day Everyone Stopped Training

When we graduated from primary school, we stared training with adults from 6pm to 8pm, three times a week. In these sessions, there was no time dedicated to basics—it was only *ji-geiko*. However, we always started with *kirikaeshi* and ended with *uchikomi*, *kakari-geiko* and *kirikaeshi*. There were probably about one hundred people training at the dojo, adults and teenagers together. Of course, not everyone could do *ji-geiko* at the same time, so we lined up to practise with the sensei. We even had to compete to line up!

It is easy to imagine how vigorous and noisy the dojo was, but one day something weird happened. I was in a queue waiting for my turn to practise with a sensei. Gradually, the sound of *shinai* clashing faded out, and *kiai* decreased, too. Eventually, there was total silence except for two people who remained doing *ji-geiko*. Tsurumaru-sensei and Murayama-sensei, a 9-dan and an 8-dan and both graduates of the famous Budō Senmon Gakkō (Budo Vocational School), were sparring. This is not something we could see every day. As a matter of fact, this is the only *ji-geiko* that I saw between them.

I remember that Tsurumaru-sensei was doing *ji-geiko* exactly the way he always did. He did not look nervous, or even appear to be overflowing with *kiai*. He looked normal. Murayama-sensei appeared calm as well, but he was attacking without hesitation when executing his strikes. Tsurumaru-sensei was just counterattacking in exactly the way he would do to us beginners. I was a teenager at that time, I think 3-dan, but I knew that something incredible was going on right in front of my eyes.

Tsurumaru-sensei once said…"You've got to do *ji-geiko* at a level that is a little higher than your opponent, so they think they can reach you. But when they improve, you should raise your level a little higher. Repeat that and your students will, without thinking, train hard and improve their skills. You should then be able to maintain your style of kendo against whoever your opponent is."

Given who his opponent was, I probably saw his ideal kendo at that day…

Kendo That Cultivates People

by Sumi Masatake (Hanshi 8-dan) Translated by Honda Sōtarō

Part 13 Grading Examinations

The *dan* rank and *shōgō* title systems have a long history and they still play an important role in kendo today by providing practitioners with goals to work towards, and recognition of their efforts made in achieving those goals. Even though there are set criteria for grading examinations, it is difficult to ensure the validity of grading results, as judgements may be arbitrary or subjective. The stipulated length of training time required for each grade is indicated by a certain number of years, but no indication is given to the frequency or type of training required. It is difficult to say whether today's established system of grading criteria makes a valid assessment of a practitioner's skills, and it may be difficult for the grading panel to provide clear explanations of their decisions.

Most practitioners of kendo aim for a higher grade, and those who are not interested in *dan* ranks or *shōgō* titles are few and far between. Grading is not the ultimate purpose of kendo but, more than success in *shiai*, promotion is an achievable aim for practitioners who pursue correct training. Instructors who support their students' ambitions to grade have an important role. This article addresses the responsibilities of high graded practitioners involved in making judgements at grading examinations.

The establishment and purposes of the *dan* rank and *shōgō* title systems

The *dan* rank and *shōgō* title systems were incorporated into kendo when the Dai-Nippon Butokukai was established in 1895. Although there have been some modifications to the systems since their incorporation, they have played an important role in the development and diffusion of kendo over the years. The current regulations were implemented in April 2002 after a thorough investigative review was conducted in March 2001. Some examples of the revised points are:

—Further clarification of the requirements of each *dan* rank and *shōgō* title.
—Improvement of judging standards by the introduction of a selection system for judges that will also ensure better consideration of the regulations by individual judges.
—Representation of the grading levels as steps in a practitioner's kendo 'education'.
—Further clarification for practitioners of what is involved in the grading process so that they may train and develop their skills more effectively.

In addition, extra criteria were inserted into *dan* rank and *shōgō* title regulations, and grading examiners' viewpoints have been stipulated in an attempt to further clarify grading requirements.

A grading rank awarded in kendo must be proof of a practitioner's technical and mental ability as demonstrated on the day of the grading examination, although the candidate's degree of mastery is judged to a certain extent by the subjective evaluation of the examiner. Under regulated grading time and conditions, technical skill is not something that can be ascertained solely by a checklist of criteria, and so examiners also rely on their own personal experience in making judgements. This is a very difficult task, as the examiner must judge whether the candidate's skills have reached the appropriate level for promotion whilst the candidate spars against others of similar experience and skill. It is therefore essential that examiners, court examiners and the chief examiner, all have a thorough understanding of the grading criteria to ensure both fairness and validity in their judgements. Examiners also have a responsibility to study so that grading examinations are appropriately managed; this encourages practitioners to do their best and promotes the development of kendo in greater society. Therefore the Examiners Selection Committee's task of choosing appropriate judges for grading panels has wide ramifications.

To be able to consistently judge in a fair and strict manner, judges must develop their abilities through their own *keiko*, fully understand the criteria, and know where to direct their attention and gaze. Examiners should also realise that their duty lies not only in grading candidates on the day, but they also have the extra duty of upholding the standards of kendo for all practitioners in general. They should undertake their duties with an honest and sincere attitude, and should be able to explain their judgements with confidence and pride. Acts such as favouritism must be avoided at all costs. Moreover, examiners must try to gain the trust of those they are judging through their demeanour and bearing.

The grading panel's accountability for its decisions

The current regulations do not require grading examiners to be accountable for their judgements. In Japan, a large number of practitioners attend the six 6-dan, five 7-dan and two 8-dan examinations held each year, and even if the grading venue is divided into several courts, it is almost impossible for the examiners to make proper records of each candidate's technical performance. However, I do not think this is the case for smaller *shodan* to 5-dan examinations which take place in each prefecture, and I wonder if we can improve the current method of providing candidates with feedback on their evaluation.

The examiners concentrate on the candidate's performance in *tachiai* and record their overall judgement. Even when a candidate receives a 'pass' there is still generally some room for improvement, as the result does not necessarily mean their performance was 'perfect'. Also in the case of a candidate receiving a 'fail', he or she may not know why they failed. In either case candidates may not know what areas of their kendo is lacking, and so will not know what to focus on in future *keiko*.

Many candidates, especially those attempting *shodan* to 3-dan examinations, may not have yet comprehended the technical structure of kendo or which skills are necessary for further development. Most inexperienced practitioners are still simply trying out the techniques that they have been taught against an opponent. Even if they are aware of which of their strikes are successful, or when they have been struck successfully, often they are overlooking certain aspects of their posture, attire or etiquette (*reihō*), or simply lack maturity in their basic techniques or a fullness of spirit (*kisei*).

Examiners have only sixty seconds to make a judgement about a candidate's *tachiai* and there is not really enough time to record technical details of each performance. It would be ideal, however, if each candidate could receive feedback from judges to provide them with training goals, irrespective of having passed or failed. If a candidate is experiencing some technical difficulty, it is usually a result of their regular *keiko* and not something that happened randomly on the day of the grading.

I have been appointed as the chairman of a kendo association in the area of the prefecture in which I live, and in this capacity I provide practitioners who take their 1-*kyū* grading with the following material for feedback after their examination. Four of the five examiners are assigned a specific point to evaluate (see below). The fifth examiner is a court examiner who comes from another town or city and is in charge of the grading panel. Firstly, each examiner makes an overall judgement of the candidates. Secondly, they tick which items they think each candidate needs to work on. A separate piece of paper is provided for each point.

* * *

1-kyū Examination Feedback

Point A: Etiquette / Attire

- [ ] Adjust the length of your *himo* (*men*/*dō*/*kote*) and tie them properly. The *men-himo* should not be longer than 40 cm.
- [ ] Smooth out your *keiko-gi* so that it does not bunch up around your back. The front hem of your *hakama* should not be raised up.
- [ ] The *nakayui* should be tied at a point one-quarter from the top of the total length of the *shinai*.
- [ ] You should not take your eyes off your opponent when you perform the standing bow (*ritsurei*) before and after your *tachiai*.
- [ ] Keep your posture straight when performing *sonkyo*.

Point B: *Kamae* / Footwork / Basics

- [ ] The *tsuka-gashira* should not be visibly protruding from the bottom of your left hand nor should the *shinai* be held in a perpendicular fashion as if gripping a hammer.
- [ ] The height and direction of your *kensen* should vary with respect to your opponent's chest and throat area.
- [ ] Both feet should be parallel and pointing straight forwards in the direction of your opponent and your left heel should be slightly raised.
- [ ] In the lead-up to and the aftermath of an attack you should use small and quick *okuri-ashi*; do not walk with normal *ayumi-ashi* steps.
- [ ] Keep your upper body vertically straight when striking and use strong *fumikomi*.

Point C: *Kirikaeshi*

- [ ] Give a big and deep shout from your stomach at *tōma* distance before moving in to make the initial *shōmen* strike.
- [ ] When you swing your *shinai* up, the *furikaburi* motion should bring your left hand up and clearly above your face.
- [ ] Stretch both arms forward when making the initial *shōmen* strike; do not raise them unnecessarily.
- [ ] Strike *sayū-men* with appropriate distancing so that the *monouchi* section of the *shinai* strikes your partner's *men*. The strikes should be made at an angle of 45 degrees.
- [ ] Maintain your *kiai* in one breath for as long as you can; ideally until the final *shōmen* strike.

Point D: *Gokaku-geiko*

- [ ] Strike correctly with correct posture; it is unacceptable to lean your back and shoulders forward into your attack. You must be facing your opponent square-on at all times.
- [ ] Attempt to attack all of the three main targets (*men*, *dō* and *kote*); just focusing on making *men* strikes is insufficient.
- [ ] Do not always stop after making one attacking motion; continue with *nidan-waza* and *renzoku-waza*.
- [ ] Try to use a bigger *kiai* than your opponent and show a stronger fighting spirit. You are not likely to pass if you are shy or hesitant.
- [ ] Do not block just for the sake of blocking; follow up with a counter-attack.

* * *

After the grading results are announced on the day, all candidates receive their evaluation sheets that provide them with feedback and identify which areas of their kendo they need to work on. They are not informed which examiner provided the information so some anonymity is maintained. If candidates receive three or more cautions by three or more examiners, they will fail; however they can keep the evaluation sheets and show them to their kendo teacher. Over time this system has increased the percentage of candidates who pass.

Gradings are an important opportunity for practitioners to gauge their progress and receive recognition for their efforts, so strictness and fairness must be ensured. If the grading system as a whole is to contribute to the betterment of kendo, then I feel that candidates require appropriate feedback, examiners' judging skills must be kept sharp, and

grading ethics must be impeccable. As candidates are paying examination fees, I would suggest that examiners have a professional responsibility in how they use their knowledge and expertise, and should therefore be held accountable for their decisions.

I was invited to be on a grading panel in Europe, and on one occasion I saw a failed candidate approach one of the examiners and modestly ask what mistakes he had been making. The examiner kindly obliged and used the notes he had taken to answer the candidate's inquiry. I was pleased to see how they both discussed the matter so congenially. I could see that the examinee had accepted his failure and was simply hoping to find out which areas he should improve on; practitioners will not improve by dwelling on negative results or blaming their teachers. It was an exchange of mutual respect for each other's positions and opinions, and I felt it was indicative of their personal characters and the culture of their nation. It also demonstrated the examiner's sense of accountability for his decisions.

The notion of 'accountability' has started to be used more and more often in Japan recently. Grading panelists are in a position to use their specialist knowledge to make accessible interpretations of regulations for the benefit of examinees. Justifiable decisions and the publication of those decisions are an important part of accountability. The text found in regulations is often abstract and only so much can be transmitted by words. Each judge must analyse and clearly understand the current regulations and appropriately apply them in making their decisions so that candidates can benefit from the grading experience. At the prefectural and local level, there have been many instances where booklets have been published that include descriptions of technical points for examinees and summaries of technical contents for instructors.

There was a time when the population of children practising kendo increased explosively, but this is no longer the case today. I feel that we would see a marked improvement in the overall quality of kendo if we implemented a standardised system for providing grading candidates with detailed feedback on their performance.

Here are two *tanka* poems about kendo…
 "These days there is much ado about shiai, while shinsa linger in the corner shadows."

This does not paint a bright future for kendo.
 "Victory is here today and gone tomorrow, yet there is no end to the path of self-improvement."

Instil this advice in your students' minds and have them train hard.

The Kendo Coach
Sports Psychology in Kendo

Part 8 — Aggression in Kendo: part 3

By Blake Bennett

"Yanagita Ganjiro completed the two-hundred-match seigan on the final day of his thousand-day training period. He then practiced five hundred more days in a row and undertook the three-day, six-hundred-match seigan. Blows received from the short, thick Muto-ryū bamboo sword (shinai) were extremely painful. Yanagita recalled: "After the first day my head was full of lumps and my body covered with bruises, but I did not feel weak. On the second day I began to suffer. I thought I would have to give up halfway. I managed to continue and near the end of the day I experienced 'selflessness' – I naturally blended with my opponent and moved in unhindered freedom. Although my spirit was strong my body was weak. My urine was dark red and I had no appetite. Nevertheless, I passed the final day's contests with a clear mind; I felt as if I was floating among the clouds."

(Stevens, 1984)

Introduction
—The Development of the Character via Harsh Training

As discussed in the previous articles, definitions of aggression and violence within a sporting context depend heavily on the intent of the aggressor. Difficult to ascertain, further complexities arise when considering the intrinsic aggression/violence evident in contact sports and combat arts such as kendo. Furthermore, consideration must be given to the assessment of behaviours as either sanctioned or unsanctioned, or even as a result of player norms within different dojo.

Without the immediate ability to determine the intent of either practitioner, one may consider how a first time spectator of kendo is often struck by the aggressive and violent appearance of *zanshin*, *kiai*, or a fighter's general mannerisms—undoubtedly compounded by the display of common techniques such as *taiatari* and *tsuki*—as the origin of kendo as a form of combat naturally reveals a fierce intensity between each practitioner as they attack each other with bamboo swords.

However despite its outwardly aggressive appearance, the All Japan Kendo Federation (AJKF) insists that the practice of kendo encompasses and emphasises a number of moral and ethical principles, therefore endorsing its value as a means of physical, mental and cultural education. In this respect, the following article will examine the goal to merge physical education and ethical education within such an extreme form of physical pursuit, by investigating the "Concept and Purpose of Kendo" (AJKF, 1975) and the "Mindset of Kendo Instruction" (AJKF, 2007). Using these documents as a basis for discussion regarding the proclaimed holistic and social value of kendo participation, Eastern concepts of the mind-body relationship, and the ideas behind *shugyō* (ascetic practice), *keiko* (training), *jōge-kankei* (hierarchical relations), *kitae* (forging), and *shitsuke* (manners) will also be considered in an attempt to cover a majority of the rationales and justifications of the unique teaching methods utilised in kendo.

The overall aim of this, and my next few articles, will be to uncover factors that when compiled, create a drive in the kendo student to willingly undergo and tolerate ongoing harsh training methods based on trust and their acceptance of the exacting pedagogical methods as an important tool in his or her complete character development.

The Dissemination of Correct Kendo

1a. "The Concept and Purpose of Kendo"

With the steady growth of kendo on an international scale since the 1960s, the AJKF has gone to great lengths to document and promote the idea of correct, Japanese kendo. In this respect, the objective of ensuring kendo training is understood and promoted as a means to cultivate the body and mind, as well as a vehicle for ethical and spiritual education, the "Concept and Purpose of Kendo" was developed in 1975—a reaction to the overt "sportification" of kendo in the post war period.

The basis of the "Concept of Kendo" states that, through the practice of kendo, one should aim to discipline his/her character through the application of the principles of the *katana* (sword). Expressing the importance of the rigid training required in order to achieve a level of proficiency, it continues:

> *The purpose of practicing Kendo is:*
> *To mould the mind and body,*
> *To cultivate a vigorous spirit,*
> *And through correct and rigid training,*
> *To strive for improvement in the art of Kendo,*
> *To hold in esteem human courtesy and honour,*
> *To associate with others with sincerity,*
> *And to forever pursue the cultivation of oneself.*
> *This will make one be able:*
> *To love his/her country and society,*
> *To contribute to the development of culture*
> *And to promote peace and prosperity among all peoples.*

The reference to "correct and rigid training" in the passage above undoubtedly refers to the importance of accurate (correct) technique, whilst rigid training—with the focus of "moulding the mind and body" and "to cultivate a vigorous spirit"—more than likely includes reference to the enhancement of power, agility, reaction time, and anaerobic and aerobic efficiency and mental toughness necessary for prolonged participation.

As in any sport or physical pursuit, a necessity exists for varying methods of sport-specific, intensive physical training to take place in order to develop the body's energy systems required for optimal performance. The principles of specificity and over-loading are basic premises in sport physiology, and the implementation of rigorous exercise in kendo training thus abides by these training principles.

However with regards to the topic of this discussion, although it may be true that the content of regular trainings must be increasingly physically challenging in order for a young kendo practitioner to enhance his/her physical ability, the way in which a *motodachi* works to facilitate this objective can sometimes result in ambiguous behaviour. Such behaviour may fall within a grey area between *kitae*, aggression/violence, and, depending on intent/frequency/manipulation of power imbalances, may also teeter on *ijime* (bullying). I will discuss this point further in a later article regarding *kitae* and *shitsuke*.

The latter half of the AJKF's document seeks to depict kendo training as a means to develop or cultivate oneself in a moralistic sense. As a typical model of many sports charters (e.g. the Olympic Charter, 2007), the "Concept of Kendo" is a declaration of intrinsic values that encourage the training of one's mind and body to polish one's art, character, and way of life in order to benefit society.

In accordance with the "Purpose of Kendo", the intent of the kendo practitioner should be to "hold in esteem human courtesy and honour" in order to "promote peace and prosperity." However, a paradox exists between the ideals of modern kendo as a holistic and positive pursuit for overall human and societal development, versus aggressive approaches and misuse of the *shinai*—predominantly dictated by tradition, club customs, and player norms—by some people during harsh training methods like *kakari-geiko*. Therefore, as attitudes change towards traditional teaching methods, the issue of how modern Japanese society interprets this paradox, and particularly the way the kendo community outside of Japan practises correct Japanese kendo as it continues its international dissemination, is an important consideration.

As Hurst (1998) and Sumi (2006) observe, kendo's function as a tool for spiritual development, character-building and enhanced morality, in addition to instilling discipline and reviving an interest in traditional values through the means of combat orientated training methods, are of utmost importance for modern youth. As such, an instructor's objective to forge the character of the student for their overall benefit is pure and good in many. However, the continuation and desire to uphold traditional customs and player norms—specifically, aggressive traditions—poses many potential issues to the survival of aggressive kendo clubs in a society (both in Japan and abroad) with ever changing views.

1b. "The Mindset of Kendo Instruction"

Aimed at providing a set of guiding principles for the instruction of kendo, the "Mindset of Kendo Instruction" was developed by the AJKF in 2007. Somewhat conceptual in content, it resembles an idealistic format espoused by many other sporting charters promoting respect for others, health and safety, and adherence to the techniques and rules of the activity. Important to this discussion of aggression in kendo are the sections regarding *reihō* (etiquette) and *shōgai kendō* (lifelong kendo).

The importance of *reihō* in kendo is such that, regardless of the competitive element of the bout, it is considered central to instruction that forms of etiquette and manners are emphasised in order to nurture people with a dignified and humane character. Also, by maintaining a positive attitude towards etiquette, it is believed that the practitioner can develop a modest attitude to life and realise the ideal of *kōken-chiai* (the desire to achieve mutual understanding and betterment of humanity through kendo) (AJKF, 2007).

Second, the section regarding lifelong kendo states that through instruction in kendo training, "Students should be encouraged to apply the full measure of care to issues of safety and health" (AJKF, 2007). It is suggested that through training in kendo, one may be able to develop a richer outlook on life and, by putting the culture of kendo into practice outside the dojo, increase his/her social vigour (AJKF, 2007).

As these documents show, the objectives of kendo training and competition are aimed at the betterment of the practitioner's character. Stating terms such as "courtesy and honour", "peace and prosperity", "*kōken-chiai*"(mutual respect through crossing swords), and "a dignified and humane character", kendo practice is intended to raise a set of moralistic values that work to enhance mankind, and thus benefit society at large. In this way, as the elements of both etiquette and safety are described as essential in the dojo, modern kendo training should be far removed from any intent to cause an opponent physical or psychological harm; allowing aggressive behavior directly contradicts the recommended ideal mindset of an instructor.

However, according to the findings of a survey conducted into this topic, although understanding and endeavours to promote these ideals espoused by the AJKF, many Japanese kendo instructors consider there to be a number of instances where violence is present within training (i.e. *mukae-zuki* where the tip of the *shinai* is thrust into the throat of the attacker as they move in to strike), according to their individual interpretations of violence. This in turn suggests that the 'full measure of care of safety and health' is lacking at certain times. This

is not to imply that instructors are careless in their approaches; however, it raises the question as to why certain types of aggressive customs are allowed to continue, despite the obvious unethical nature of violence contradicting the purposes of kendo participation. This concern will be further examined throughout the remainder of this series of articles.

2. The Eastern Concept of the Body and Mind Relationship in Keiko

To better understand the importance placed on extremely rigorous physical training in kendo with the goal of holistic cultivation, Eastern concepts regarding the relationship between body and mind—and the forging or tempering thereof—deserves explanation.

Japanese philosophy, as heavily influenced by neo-Confucian and Buddhist thought, suggests that the body shelters or houses the mind or spirit (Yuasa 1990; Hurst, 1998). An idea that opposes Western dualistic philosophy that typically views the mind and body as separate entities (Yuasa, 1990), Eastern thought in this area suggests that through dedicated and repetitious physical training in the prescribed *kata* forms of *geidō*, the process of the Mutō-ryū's *seigan*, or *kakari-geiko* in terms of modern kendo training, bears no distinction between the physical development of the body, and the cultivation of the mind and spirit. Rather, by accepting the unified correlation of each, this understanding of the body-mind/mind-body relationship suggests that the mind can be cultivated and even enlightened through rigorous physical training (Yuasa 1987; Hurst, 1998). Examples of terms used in many forms of *geidō* that illustrate this point are *shinshin-ittai* (mind and body as one) and *shinshin-ichinyo* (mind and body are the same) (Hurst, 1998, p.191).

As Eastern thought regarding the mind-body relationship considers each to be inextricably linked, it is through the tempering or forging of the body with an attitude of *sutemi* (absolute conviction to an attack/self-sacrifice) by way of training methods such as *kirikaeshi* and *kakari-geiko* that one may achieve mental strength in the form of confidence, and realise the virtues of humility, patience and *kisei* (will power) (Sumi, 2006). As such, it is an underlying mindset in the kendo dojo that, via means of rigorous training aided by the important role of the *motodachi* (receiver), an attacker's physical limits are constantly pushed in order to achieve these benefits. Thus, by applying physical power to the attacker to deny insufficient attacks, and pressure (e.g. *seme*) to test concentration, the role of the *motodachi* is to

provide productive training to guide the attacker to their physical and mental potential (Sumi, 2006).

Sumi suggests that these types of harsh training regimens are to be ongoing in the youngster's journey as they are effectively challenged to dig deep for the mental resolve to overcome their discomfort, forming a strong and resolute spirit that leads to a high level of future technical and mental fortitude.

3. Shugyō and Keiko

During the course of their training, students of the various traditional Tokugawa *ryūha* (martial art schools) were expected to undergo exhausting training regimes to challenge themselves physically, thus developing the mental fortitude necessary to acquire the ideal state of mind of a warrior (Hurst, 1998). The way in which this was achieved was through a process known as *shugyō* (ascetic training), as the student deprived himself of luxuries and undertook endeavours, such as that described by Miyamoto Musashi as "*sennichi no tan, mannichi no ren*" (one thousand days of forging, ten thousand days of training).

A more common term used in *geidō* throughout medieval and early modern times with the similar objective of *shugyō*—to forge the body and therefore cultivate the ideal state of mind within the context of a journey—was that of *keiko*. A word initially deriving from the term *keiko-shōkon* meaning "to reflect upon past ways to shed light on the present" (Hurst, 1998, p. 194), the objectives of *keiko* took on a predominantly physical nature in medieval times, with a focus on engaged and holistic learning through repetition of the *kata*.

3a. Seigan

Perhaps one of the most dramatic forms of swordsman *keiko/shugyō* is known as *seigan*, and was developed by Yamaoka Tesshū, founder of the Ittō Shōden Mutō-ryū (Donohue, 1991). Divided into three stages, the first tier of training required the practitioner to undergo a rigorous regime of 1000 days continuous practice—upon completion of which, he would face a total of 200 opponents in consecutive bouts. Stopping only for food and toilet breaks, the practitioner was not allowed to sit or rest for the duration of the test, and only after completion of this gruelling exercise was he eligible to attempt the second stage of *seigan*.

The second stage took place following a further 500-day training regime, and was conducted over three successive days involving a total of 600 matches. It was only after completion of the second stage that one was able to attempt the third and final level of *seigan*—a 7-day ordeal that required the practitioner to undergo 1400 consecutive bouts.

Tesshū asserted that *seigan* "Should lead to the heart of things, where one can directly confront life and death" (Stevens, 1984, p. 25), and Donohue (1991) suggests that the motivation behind such severe training methods was to exhaust all of the practitioner's physical stamina and technique, so that it is only the power of the spirit that allows him to raise his sword for yet another bout. In this way one may see the strong element of attitudinal or spiritual meaning in the process of *shugyō* and/or *keiko*; therefore, linking each to *kokoro-gamae* (mental attitude) concerning the way in which one should live his life (Hurst, 1998).

Among other aspects such as an emphasis on continual and almost monotonous practice of the basics, Donohue suggests that the all-pervasive idea that swordsmanship is primarily the training of the spirit through harsh methods in *shugyō* and *keiko*, are the modern kendo practitioner's inheritance from Tesshū's legacy. As Donohue phrased it, referring to both past and present thought in the art of the sword, harsh physical training during *keiko/shugyō* is the road to spiritual mastery.

3b. Kan-geiko—Winter Training

A modern-day training environment created with the same objective of forging the participant under the harshest of conditions, is that of *kan-geiko* (winter training). Running for different durations (sometimes several weeks) and starting at varying times depending on the dojo, *kan-geiko* is typically carried out from the very early hours of the morning in the coldest time of winter. Notorious for the forms of rough training methods employed on the young participants by older more experienced practitioners, the *kan-geiko* event has met increasing opposition regarding its function as a way to improve skill in kendo; the students participating are generally pushed to exhaustion by their *motodachi*, and are rarely given any recovery time. However, advocates of the *kan-geiko* experience insist on its holistic value, and as an important part of cultivating a strong character in modern youth through training with *motodachi* of older generations.

In an article concerning the spiritual development and strengthening of modern youth, Sakudō (2007) offers the following interpretations of the purpose of *kan-geiko*:

"At a glimpse, one may speculate about the significance of the seemingly irrational and 'un-scientific' practice of *kan-geiko*. On the exterior, such an event may be misconstrued as 'a lesson in bullying', however to phrase in Buddhist terms, it is essentially the act of leaving the 'good/comfortable life' (everyday life) behind. As such, for those who commute each morning and for those who stay on site, regular daily and societal routines are indeed left behind. It is a time when, in bitterly cold conditions, participants sacrifice body and soul whilst pushing the limits of their physical ability and mental resolve. One way to view this form of training is not simply a means to improve technical skill, but rather, it could be considered as 'a means to question the true and rational way to live as a human being.'

When one contemplates the duality of pleasure and pain, it may be said that instances where we as humans seek to avoid challenging/harsh conditions in lieu of pleasure and luxuries are, in a word, spreading. In this sense, the *kan-geiko* environment becomes a place where one may directly face his weaknesses, skewer this dual sense of pain and pleasure, and begin to nurture a spirit strong enough to live a happy life. Herein lays the significance of *kan-geiko*."(Sakudō, 2007, pp. 261-262)

In line with the literature examined in Part 1 and 2 of this series concerning the issue of intent, Sakudō continues by outlying the ideal intents of the *motodachi* during this rigorous process as;

"1) Drawing the best from the individual qualities of the student, while at the same time, as a practitioner of kendo, concern oneself with the gradual acquisition and improvement of appropriate movement; 2) giving great consideration to the level of *kitae* (forging) used on a student, by acting in accordance to the student's overall stage of ability; and, 3) carefully considering the importance of developing the idyllic connection/rapport with the student."

Assuming these three objectives are maintained, particularly harsh training in *kan-geiko* can be said to fall in line with the ideals of the "Mindset of Kendo Instruction"—making it simply an assertive way to instill the objectives of kendo training. Sakudō reasons,

"This forging (of the children and students) and training (for sensei and sempai) brings about a harmony between each person as one discovers a level of training that he cannot achieve by himself, and as such, a feeling of gratitude develops. While denying the opponent any respite, a sense of affirmation is achieved within the confrontational relationship between *motodachi* and *kakarite*—a 'prickly' process through which *kōken-chiai* is created. This is how *kan-geiko* works to nurture a person strong of will." He then concludes by stating that,

"In a modern society where one is apt to neglect the relationships between his fellow man, and the natural world around him, the objective of *kan-geiko* acts to restore this contact, while facilitating the regeneration of a soft skinned being to his proper, harder form." (2007, p. 262)

In my next article, the issues of *kitae* and *shitsuke* (discipline) will be covered in an attempt to show how the objective of polishing the mind is facilitated. Also, on the basis of a moralistic approach to harsh training for holistic development, the use of *jōge-kankei* and the idea of *kōken-chiai* will be further considered for their role of ensuring the on-going guidance and leadership of younger members within the norms of the club. Overall, the various aspects of kendo that generate a motivation in the student to willingly undergo and tolerate ongoing harsh training methods will be examined.

References

- AJKF, "Concept of Kendo". Retrieved July 1, 2010, from http://www.kendo.or.jp/news/img/kokorogamae/20070314_kokorogamae.pdf
- "The Mindset of Kendo Instruction"(2007). Retrieved July 1, 2010, from http://www.kendo.or.jp/news/img/kokorogamae/20070314_kokorogamae.pdf
- Baron, R.A. & Richardson, D.R. (1994). *Human aggression*. New York, NY: Plenum Press.
- Bredemeier, B.J. & Shields, D.L. (2008). *Moral Reasoning in the Context of Sport*. Retrieved August 28, 2010 from http://tigger.uic.edu/~lnucci/MoralEd/articles.html
- Carron, A.V. (1984). *Motivation: Implications for Coaching and Teaching*. London: Sports Dynamics.
- Donohue, J.J. (1991). *The forge of the spirit: structure, motion, and meaning in the Japanese martial tradition*. New York, NY: Garland Publishing, Inc.
- Dunn, J.G. & Dunn, J. C. (1999). "Goal orientation, perceptions of aggression, and sportspersonship in elite male youth ice hockey players".*The Sport Psychologist*, 13, pp. 183-200.
- Gallucci, N.T. (2008). *Sport Psychology: Performance Enhancement, Performance Inhibition, Individuals, and Teams*. New York, NY: Psychology Press.
- Geen, R.G. (2001). *Human Aggressiveness*. (2nd ed.). Milton Keynes: Open University Press.
- Gill, D.L. & Williams, L. (2008).*Psychological Dynamics of Sport and Exercise* (3rd ed.). Champaign, IL: Human Kinetics.
- Hurst, C. (1998). *Armed Martial Arts of Japan: Swordsmanship and Archery*. London: Yale University Press.
- IOC, "Olympic Charter" (2007). Retrieved January 28, 2010, from http://www.joc.or.jp/olympism/charter/
- Kerr, J.H. (2005). *Rethinking Aggression and Violence in Sport*. New York, NY: Routledge.
- "Killing Causes Kendō Club to Call it Quits". (1999, October 23). *Mainichi Shimbun*. Retrieved October 13, 2010, from http://www.accessmylibrary.com/article-1G1-56898494/killing-causes-kendō-club.html
- LeUnes, A.D. & Nation, J.R. (1989). *Sport psychology: an introduction*. Chicago: Nelson-Hall Inc.
- Levin, D., Smith, E., Caldwell, L. & Kimbrough, J. (1995)."Violence and high school sports participation". *Pediatric Exercise Science*, 7, pp. 379-388.
- Nakamura, R.M. (1996). *The Power of Positive Coaching*. Sudbury, Massachusetts; Jones and Bartlett Publishers.
- Sakudō Masao, (2007). "Kendō wo tsūjite utare-tsuyosa wo hagukumu", *Jidō Shinri 2*, 845, pp. 259-263.
- Skinner, B.F. (1953). "Science and human behavior". Oxford, England: Macmillan.
- Stevens, J. (1984). *The Sword of No-sword: Life of the Warrior Master Tesshū*. Boston: Shambala.
- Sumi Masatake (2006). *Hito wo Sodateru Kendō*. Tokyo, Nippon Budokan.
- Tucker, L.W. & Parks, J.B. (2001). "Effects of gender and sport type on intercollegiate athletes' perceptions of the legitimacy of aggressive behaviour in sport". *Sociology of Sport Journal*, 18, pp. 403-413.
- Yuasa Yasuo, (Kasulis, T. P. & Nagatomo Shigenori trans.) (1990). *The Body: Toward an Eastern Mind*. Kodansha; Tokyo.

A Budo Camp on the Black Sea

By Ivayla Ivanova

People wearing *hakama*, with *katana* tucked in their *obi*, walked along the path next to the ocean. But this is not a scene taken from a new samurai movie: it was actually the sight of the participants of "The Art of the Japanese Sword" Summer Budo Camp on their way to training. For the third year in row, this budo camp took place from August 11-19, 2012, on the sea shore near Varna, Bulgaria. It was organised by the Bulgarian Kendo Federation and Varna Free University Chernorizets Hrabur. This year's group of participants who came from Bulgaria, Germany, Russia and France, were able to train in iaido, jodo and kendo.

The instructors at the camp were;
- **Alexander Arabadzhiev**—Kendo 6-dan, the highest rank in Bulgaria, and President of the Bulgarian Kendo Federation.
- **Francois Delage**—Kendo 6-dan from France, Technical Director of the Aquitaine region.
- **Karl Dannecker**—Iaido 6-dan, jodo 6-dan, President of the German Jodo Federation.

Two-hour training sessions for each discipline were held every day at the wonderful training facilities of Varna Free University. The more dedicated practitioners even went to the beach for warming up at sunrise.

The main idea of the camp is for practitioners of kendo, iaido and jodo to gather in one place, not just for practice, but to also have some rest and recreation at a Black Sea resort area. Sometimes we forget that we are one big family under the umbrella of the International Kendo Federation. However, living and training together in kendo, iaido and jodo during this camp reminded us that we are all friends walking along the same path. Furthermore, when we go somewhere for a seminar, our family members and friends usually stay at home. However, at this camp, each participant was encouraged to bring children, parents, friends or spouses in order for all to have a nice time together.

If you visit Varna and Bulagria, and would like to join us for kendo and iaido practice during your stay, please contact Kaiseikan Dojo:
- Leonid Karavaev (+359 879 387 877 or leonid.karavaev@gmail.com);
- Dojo secretary Ivayla Ivanova (+359 887 650 598); or visit our website (http://www.kaiseikan.com).

Fostering the 'Gut Instinct'

By Taylor Winter (Otago University)

Decision making is an essential skill in kendo, as it is in every facet of life. There are two types of decision making process—intuitive and analytical—and both have distinct differences and importance in modern decision making models. By not clearly understanding their similarities and differences, we can inadvertently use the two types incorrectly. I suggest in this article that this is a mistake being made by beginners who are seeking to emulate their seniors. Beginners think analytically rather than intuitively, resulting in increased reaction times and 'freezing up'. The root cause of this problem lies within the engagement between seniors and juniors during *keiko*. Junior students try to copy (model) their seniors as best as possible, but mistakenly interpret that their seniors are successful by using analytical models during *keiko*. This is arguably due to senior practitioners incorrectly engaging with beginners by displaying an analytical model of decision making.

The process of analytical decision making, as described by Hasties and Dawes (2011), first involves a thorough interpretation of a situation in order to deduce every possible course of action. The most desirable option to enact is then determined by predicting the potential outcomes from each of them. The consequences of each outcome are then inferred before finally deciding on the correct action. Clearly, this method is cognitively laden and takes time (Keeney, 1982). In kendo, this could contribute to a scenario whereby a senior strikes the beginner without the latter realising the completion of the strike. Even if the receiver blocks the strike, this might only be a reflexive block—a lower level response not requiring conscious thought.

Fostering the 'Gut Instinct'

In application, a practitioner would employ an analytical decision making model by investigating elements such as *maai* and their opponent's *kamae*. They would then be inundated with potential actions, such as 'I could strike *men*.' However, we also have preferences, possibly feeling more confident with striking *kote* instead. The consequences could be a successful *men* strike, or the opponent striking *de-gote*. In any respect, it will leave you slow to react and prone to freezing up without taking action. Therefore, this method is highly limited in functionality, and all but useless for developing the correct kendo mentality.

Fortunately our brains work in such a way that if an analytical model is inadequate, it should theoretically change to a more successful decision model. Consider when you try and turn on a television, you would only press the on/off button on the remote a few times before considering an alternative course of action to achieve the goal of turning on the television, i.e. changing the batteries. In kendo, we should see a similar change in model once beginners realise that analytical models harbour poor results in *ji-geiko*. Beginners should progressively change to a more successful model that relies more on intuition, rather than analysis.

Intuitive decision making is a more linear approach. The first interpreted view of a situation elicits an immediate action. Renowned poet and scholar Robert Graves encapsulated the essence of intuitive decision making by saying that it "cuts out all the routine processes of thought and leaps straight from the problem to the answer." A particular cue within a situation allows the recognition of a pattern (problem) which immediately activates an action (answer). The key is that there is no 'sizing up' of alternative actions; if the answer suits the framework of the problem, use it. This basic idea is embodied within the "Recognition-Primed Decision" model first introduced by Klein in 1986. If your opponent lifts their *kensen* (problem), strike *kote* (answer). Intuitive answers are always reasonable but not always perfect: if *kote* is not successful, choose the next option and strike *men*.

Practitioners of kendo who fit into the upper quartile of expertise certainly use an intuitive decision making model. Beginners use an analytical form of decision making, or 'think too much'. This is not directly taught to beginners; it is a naturally adopted method as people initially use an analytical decision making process in new situations. The lack of a more rapid shift to an intuitive model suggests that something within the framework of kendo is reinforcing an analytical model to slow down, or even halt, the attainment of an intuitive model.

Modelling is a simple process in which a person demonstrates a behaviour for others to emulate (Gleitman, Reisberg and Gross, 2007). It is possible to immediately see how this fits into the hierarchical system of kendo, but the extent to which modelling occurs can sometimes be underestimated. Beginners mimic their seniors to improve at kendo, not only by imitating motor movements, but also by attempting to copy a state of mind. Although the concept of modelling has been around since its introduction by Albert Bandura in 1977, the idea that a thought process like a decision model could be mimicked is relatively new. Subiaul, Cantlon, Holloway and Terrace (2004) introduced the term 'cognitive imitation' in their study on rhesus monkeys. They showed a cognitive rule being utilised by monkeys who had only ever observed the same rule in other monkeys, without the use of movement or vocalisation.

A similar process in humans occurs in kendo—beginners try to copy cognitive rules, i.e. decision making models from their seniors. The occurrence of cognitive imitation elicits a misinterpretation of the decision models of seniors: they are analytical rather than intuitive. Consequently, beginners try and push on using analytical decision models rather than progressing to a more successful intuitive one. In either *shiai* or *ji-geiko*, beginners need to be pushed into using intuitive models in order to better foster the correct kendo mind set. This is a primary benefit of *kakari-geiko*: a beginner is striking intuitively without superfluous analysis. However, the effect of *kakari-geiko* may be stymied due to the significantly greater effect of the modelling of senior practitioners.

As a preliminary measure, seniors must rethink how they engage with beginners. A correct intuitive model must be demonstrated in order to promote a decision model shift in beginners earlier in their kendo career. How exactly to do this can be a problematic process—it ultimately depends on the environment, and the availability of a range of senior students—for beginners to gain a more dynamic knowledge of correct cognitive patterns. Typically, seniors fall into an analytical style of *ji-geiko* when engaging against beginners. This does give beginners a chance to feel out what to do during *ji-geiko*, but ideally the middle level seniors might consider making efforts not to do this. The reason for this is that without the same significant experience of a high rank senior, a senior of middle rank just turns *ji-geiko* into a one-sided fight where they wait instead of engaging. Although the senior practitioner may have some success in this method when fighting a beginner, it may reinforce an incorrect decision model.

It seems judgemental, but seniors of middle rank may sometimes actually promote incorrect kendo by not maintaining proper engagement, and appearing to be technically superior. Perceived success with an improper decision model is then being subconsciously acknowledged by beginner and reinforced through cognitive imitation. Seniors should instead attempt to be just as aware of a beginner's movements, and have an action selected for each one, as they would with an opponent of equal or greater experience to their own, rather than passively waiting. Both seniors and beginners are using analytical models but the senior, to an extent, appears to be successful as their analytical models become more efficient. However, the efficiency of an analytical model will plateau, whereas an intuitive model continues to become more efficient. By rethinking how we engage with beginners it can accelerate their learning as well as our own. The intuitive nature of our thinking increases in tandem with that of our training partner.

These concepts should not be anything new as decision making ties in with common kendo concepts such as *mushin* and *sutemi*. It therefore seems illogical that these ideas are sometimes shunned in regular training, due only to the fact that a practitioner is facing a beginner. This is probably occurring because although concepts such as intuition appear to be cognitively passive, it requires constant online monitoring in order to train yourself to maintain the correct mental state. Ironically, when fighting a beginner it requires thought to reduce thought.

Consider decision making during training and reflect on how action selection is occurring during *keiko*. Most kendoka will be interested to find that their method of decision making can change numerous times during training. Think about when this occurs with attention to the influence an opponent has on the choice of decision model being utilised. Seniors must keep a constant awareness that they are on display, and that their actions hold significant influence in the correct attainment of basic kendo principles by beginners. A step towards mitigating decision model change can assist in keeping a consistent intuitive decision model for seniors and mediate the learning curve for beginners.

References
- Bandura, A. (1977). *Social learning theory.* (2nd ed.). Prentice Hall.
- Gleitman, H., Reisberg, D., and Gross, J. (2007). *Psychology.* (7th ed.). W. W. Norton & Company Limited.
- Hastie, R., and Dawes, R. M. (2011). *Rational choice in an uncertain world, the psychology of judgment and decision making.* Sage Publications, Inc.
- Keeney, R. (1982). "Decision analysis: An overview." *Operations Research, 30*(5), pp. 803-838.
- Klein, G. (2002). *Intuition at work: Why developing your gut instincts will make you better at what you do.* Doubleday Business.
- Klein, G. A., Calderwood, R., and Clinton-Cirocco, A. (1986). "Rapid decision making on the fireground." *Proceedings of the Human Factors and Ergonomics Society 30th Annual Meeting*, 1, pp. 576-580.
- Subiaul, F., Cantlon, J., Holloway, R., and Terrace, H. (2004). "Cognitive imitation in rhesus macaques." *Science*, 305, pp. 407-410.

交剣知愛
Kōken-chiai:
Friendship through Crossing Swords

By Kate Sylvester

Kozuno Yuka-sensei is quite an accomplished *kenshi*. A Renshi 6-dan at 31 years of age, Kozuno-sensei is the only woman training with the Okayama Police elite kendo squad. She has represented Japan in four World Kendo Championships (2003, 2006, 2009, 2012) and has won the All Japan Women's Individual Championships twice (2002, 2008), not to mention numerous other competition successes throughout her illustrious kendo career to date.

Kozuno-sensei's kendo style is sophisticated, spiritually evolved, soft yet sharp with a cutting speed so fast that as you blink she could have cut you at least once, perhaps twice. You cannot help but feel her genuine warmth and unassuming self-confidence as she enjoyably engages in conversation. From that moment in time spent with her, you may be left with the feeling that you have been touched by an angel. An angel who will spiritually kick you to the curb in the *shiai-jō* as the Japanese women's team Taishō.

Kendo World interviews the 15th World Kendo Championship (WKC) Japanese women's team Taishō, Kozuno Yuka (previously Tsubota

Yuka) on her kendo career, memorable kendo experiences and impressions of international women's kendo. As you read on you will find she is an incredible woman as she openly shares her personal growth and experiences through kendo. Kozuno-sensei's words will undoubtedly offer inspiration to kenshi of all ages and levels.

KW (Kendo World): How did you come to start kendo?
KY (Kozuno Yuka): I started kendo as a first-year elementary student at the Saidaiji Budokan which is about a 10 minute walk from where I was born. My older sister and brother practised kendo so I started naturally and we all went to the dojo together. From memory, my mother liked *hakama* so much that she encouraged us so she could dress her children up in the kendo uniforms.

Kendo was thriving in the Saidaiji area around that time. The Saidaiji Budokan had morning practice that was attended by students from elementary school age right through to adults. After morning practice, we often shared *miso* soup and rice porridge together. From a young age, I enjoyed learning kendo as I was able train with a wide range of people. I went on to continue kendo at Saidaiji Junior High School and then Saidaiji High School. I wanted to become stronger at kendo so I chose to go to the National Institute of Fitness and Sports in Kanoya, Kyushu. At the time Kanoya was number 1 in Japan and had won the All Japan University Competition consecutively. After I graduated from Kanoya, I returned to Okayama and entered the Okayama Police force.

KW: Why did you join the police force?
KY: I always wanted to become a policewoman. When I was a child I really loved the television show "*Keisatsu 24-ji*" (24-hour Police). Another reason is one day when I was lost, I was picked up by a police car and taken home. I was really impressed by their kindness.

KW: Please tell us about your most memorable kendo experience up to this point.
KY: When I was a high school 3rd year student, there was a very important match that I competed in during the Inter-High selection competition. There was an expectation that we would win, however, we dropped a match which meant that we wouldn't be able to go to the All Japan Inter-High competition. It was my dream to have a successful last performance as a high school student, and since we lost I felt, a great sense of failure. I felt that I was overly optimistic but weak in skill and spirit. Since I didn't perform well, I was left with a strong feeling of regret, and I lost a sense of myself.

At that time a former kendo teacher shared with me the saying "*fuyō no yō*" or "the importance of the unimportant". The saying also has a meaning outside of kendo which is to not focus only on what is important. Even with things that you do not think are important at this moment, you must do them with enthusiasm and care. My teacher taught me that you can understand pain and warmth in the things you think are pointless or unimportant. He also explained that you must keep striving until you are totally exhausted. Even if the result does not come, you will develop confidence in yourself. I have continued believing in these words regardless of whether I achieve good results or not.

KW: Has competing in the World Kendo Championships had an impact on your life?
KY: Competing in the World Kendo Championships has had a big impact on my life. I always knew there were many people all around the world who pursued kendo with a great passion. I recently discovered that individual countries practise kendo in their own unique way, and that they have their own style. For example, people in some countries have a propensity to do kendo to win points in *shiai*, some for the enjoyment of participation, others to study kendo while cheering on their team mates, and some countries compete with strong national pride. At the World Kendo Championships, I had an unforgettable experience when I realised that

"communication of the heart" through kendo is possible between two people regardless of differences in nationality or language.

KW: *Do you have any other memorable experiences from the World Kendo Championships that you could share with us?*

KY: Rather than a particular experience from the WKC competition itself, the experiences of attending the national training camps in the lead up to the championships left lasting memories. I was completely absorbed in the WKC at the time.

KW: *There must have been a lot of pressure to perform for Japan as team Taishō. How did you deal with the pressure?*

KY: In the team competition at the WKC I fought in the position of Sempō (2006) before taking over the Taishō position (2009, 2012). When I was Sempō, the Taishō at the time performed with absolute confidence and such greatness that I felt inadequate, and that I did not have the same capacity as she did. At that time I felt that I could not be Taishō.

There were days when I felt the pressure of being the Japanese team Taishō, and there were times when I didn't feel that weight on my shoulders. When I did feel the pressure, I would recall the word "*hiraki-naoru*" or "stand strong". I was determined to rid myself of the open space, or the weakness within. Early on in my *shiai* career, even before entering the *shiai-jō* I was the most likely to give up out of all of the competitors. Of course, all sportsmen and women know that nothing is born from giving up. I realised that, no matter what position you play in, or which country you play against, it does not change your kendo. It is best that you perform your own kendo, always. I progressed remembering the words "*hiraki-naoru*" when I needed to. It gave me the confidence to do my own kendo.

KW: *Do you feel that the level of international women's kendo is improving?*

KY: I do feel that the level of international women's kendo is improving. In particular, I think that the level of kendo etiquette, pride in how armour and attire is worn, footwork and the management of distance with the opponent (*maai*) has improved a lot.

KW: *Recently you were a panellist for the AJKF panel discussion titled "Where to from here with women's kendo". Can you tell us a little how is women's kendo progressing in Japan?*

KY: The population of women's kendo in Japan has increased due to the understanding and co-operation of family members. Until recently, many women stopped kendo after getting married. But now there are numerous women who are starting kendo with their children, and many are starting in their 30s and 40s. Perhaps the circumstances are better for women in kendo now because they are more independent, and are able to participate in kendo more freely.

KW: *Generally, women outside of Japan practise kendo as a hobby, and often in environments where there are few other women. It must be difficult for you being the only woman training in the Okayama Police elite kendo squad. How are you able to train and continue improving your kendo in an environment where the men must be stronger than you in power and speed.*

KY: In general, I think male kenshi have greater speed and power than females. To train with that power and speed, I use a 'soft technique' with a strategy where I concentrate on the timing of the attack, and on the *seme* leading up to an attack. I test effective techniques in line with my own style of *keiko*.

KW: *Other than the practical side of kendo what have you learnt during your participation?*

KY: Through kendo I have learnt etiquette, how to have an appreciative heart, how to think of others, an awareness of my environment, how to understand others, consideration of others and how to look after those around me with my best effort. I particularly like the saying "*kōken-chiai*" or "Friendship through crossing swords". I think

that by practising kendo we can learn how to communicate with and understand each other. We can also learn when we should persevere, and when there is opportunity. From kendo, I think we can learn the secret of how to live our everyday lives to the fullest.

KW: You must have encountered many ups and downs throughout your competitive career. How have you managed to maintain your motivation?

KY: At my first World Kendo Championship national selection training camp, I honestly felt that I trained the hardest against the sensei, and with the most enthusiasm and positive ambition, more so than anyone else around me. However, I didn't make the Japanese team on that campaign. As a matter of fact, since I believed that I was training harder than everyone around me, it actually meant that I was comparing myself to everyone else. From this experience I learned that it is best to practise with confidence in yourself, and not be preoccupied with comparing yourself with the others around you.

KW: Can you offer any advice on how to keep striving for improvement in kendo?

KY: There are often times when things go well, followed by periods when things don't go so well. When I was in a slump, a past teacher once taught me to strive towards "*zengo-saidan*". The meaning of these words is that it is best to not be troubled by the past, the present or the future. All we can do is our very best in this moment. This is my motivation for improvement in kendo.

From when I was an elementary school student right through to high school, I never did very well in *shiai*. I think all athletes as long as they love their sport, should set high goals using their imagination whilst maintaining a strong consciousness of wanting to become stronger. It is also important to have good training partners. Most definitely something great can be achieved if you pursue your goals with a "never give up spirit" and with "*keizoku wa chikara nari*", or "continuation becomes strength".

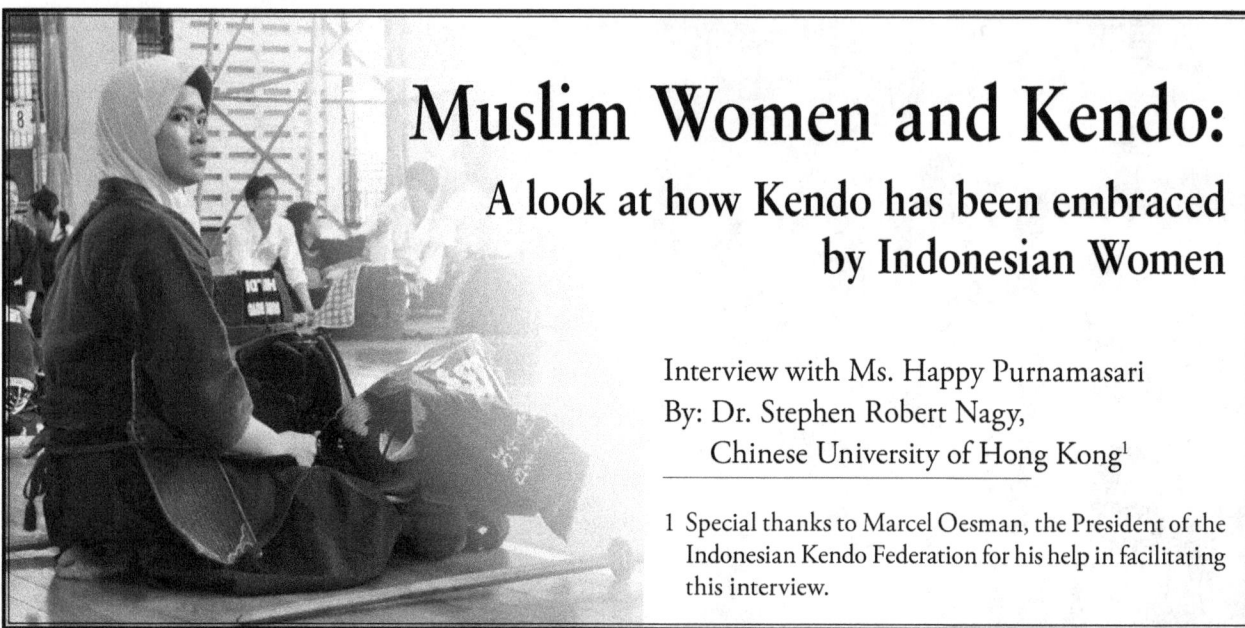

Muslim Women and Kendo:
A look at how Kendo has been embraced by Indonesian Women

Interview with Ms. Happy Purnamasari
By: Dr. Stephen Robert Nagy,
Chinese University of Hong Kong[1]

[1] Special thanks to Marcel Oesman, the President of the Indonesian Kendo Federation for his help in facilitating this interview.

Introduction

This past September, I had the opportunity to attend the "2012 Japan Matsuri" event in Jakarta, Indonesia which included as part of many events, a kendo tournament with representatives from Japan such as the President of the AJKF, Takeyasu-sensei, as well as participants from across Indonesia and neighbouring countries. It was a remarkably well organised competition with children and adult, individual and group matches.

What was particularly interesting for me was the active participation of Muslim women in the tournament. These women wore their traditional Muslim headdress and abided by their religious beliefs while at the same time participating competitively in kendo. Watching these young women in action immediately made my think about the recent London Olympics in which Ms. Wodjan Ali Seraj Abdulrahim Shaherkani, the young Saudi female judo player, became the first Saudi female to compete in an Olympic event.[2] She also had to make adjustments to her equipment to ensure that she could participate safely in the Olympic judo event while, at the same time preserve the strictures of her Islamic faith.

This short interview with Ms. Happy Purnamasari aims to provide some insight into the challenges that Muslim women face when practising kendo. Importantly though, I also hope to shed light on how Muslim women and other groups can practice kendo AND maintain their traditional beliefs.

[2] http://english.alarabiya.net/articles/2012/07/27/228681.html

(1) When did you start kendo?

My relationship with kendo goes back almost five years to 2007. Basically, there was a kendo club at my university, and the first time I saw a kendo practice I thought it was really cool. It was so interesting to see everyone wearing traditional kendo garments such as their *hakama* and *gi*. On top of that, as soon as they put on their *bōgu* and began carrying their swords, I was truly impressed. At that moment, I decided to join the kendo club.

(2) What were some of the challenges you face as a woman and Muslim with regards to kendo?

Since starting training at the end of 2007, I have never really faced any serious hurdles with regards to practising kendo or wearing my kendo uniform. At first glance, my *Jilbab*, or Muslim headpiece that women must wear appears to be a bit of a problem, but in reality it has never been a barrier. Kendo *bōgu* could be considered quite Muslim-friendly, especially for women as the *gi* and *hakama* already qualifies in covering my body in accordance to my duty as a Muslimah (Muslim woman).

I have to make some subtle adjustments to how I put my *men* on. First, I must fix my *tenugui* over my *Jilbab*. It really isn't difficult except perhaps ensuring that the fabric from the *tenugui* and the

 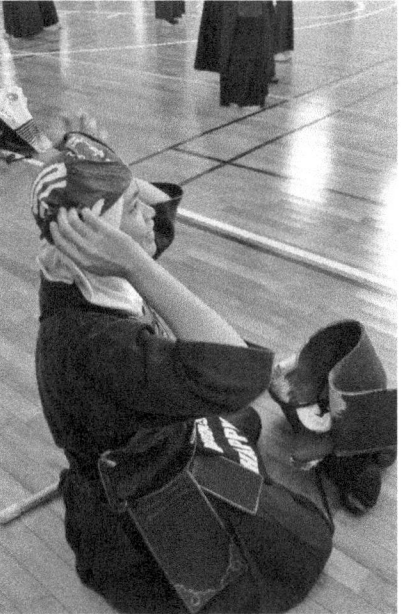 

Jilbab are firmly stuck together so that it does not slide around as I put my *men* on or during practice. It looks harder than it is. I guess you just get used to it.

Lastly, I carefully slide my *men* over my *tenugui*, tie the *himo* and start training. Again, it really isn't that difficult once you figure out how to get everything to fit together. I would also say that as a Muslim girl, I am used to my headgear so it really isn't a big issue.

(3) Was your family supportive?

When I first joined kendo, there was a time when my parents were opposed to me practising. They thought that kendo is a violent sport with hard hitting and injuries. They had more traditional beliefs of women and femininity such as cooking, dancing or other related activities. This is reasonable considering Indonesia is quite a traditional country in which men and women have very different roles in society.

That being said, I see myself as a bit of a tomboyish kind of girl, and as I grew to love kendo so much, I decided to continue even though my parents were initially quite sceptical. It was only after I had the opportunity to represent Indonesia at the ASEAN Kendo Tournament 2010 in Singapore that my parents finally agreed, and they still support me today.

(4) Are their religious challenges? How is a kendo woman viewed in religious circles?

From my understanding, there doesn't seem to be any restriction for a Muslim woman to engage in sporting activities in Muslim countries or societies. However, it must be kept in mind that Muslim women are religiously required to cover up their bodies in front of anyone who is not the husband (*Muchrim*); this includes everything except for the face and palms.

(5) What are your goals in kendo?

I practice kendo because it is an activity that I enjoy. It has become my hobby. It is a community where I meet new people and can experience another culture, and an activity that has health benefits as well. It's pretty well rounded when you think about it. In the future, I am not sure where kendo will take me, but if the past is indicative of the future, I am looking forward to it!

Bujutsu Jargon Part 3

Bruce Flanagan MA (Lecturer - Nanzan University)

Reference guide covering various bujutsu-related terminology.

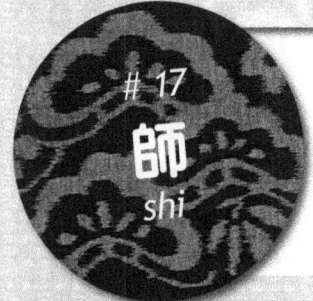

Instructor of a scholarly field, art or craft. The *shi* may be a professional who makes a living from teaching but students do not use *shi* as a direct form of address; the term *shishō* (師匠) is used which is similar to 'master'. Nowadays *shishō* can still be used when referring to those holding a position of seniority or experience. Sensei (先生) technically means those who were born before us and also functions as a polite form of address similar to 'mister' when unsure of age or rank.

Menkyo means 'license' or 'certification' and *kaiden* means being taught everything about an art or discipline. Hence the term *menkyo-kaiden* refers to certification given by a *shi* to their *deshi* to acknowledge that the *deshi* has been fully instructed in all aspects of the art or discipline in question. *Menkyo-kaiden* are still common in *koryū* (old style) schools of martial and performing arts.

Munen means to be free of delusions and preconceptions and *musō* refers to an unthinking state in which the individual is free of conscious thought. Together the two words form the Buddhist maxim *munen-musō*, which is the ideal mental state a practitioner can strive for in a given discipline. *Munen-musō* is often correlated with the term *mushin* (no-mind) which carries the extra connotations of being non-judgemental, undistracted, and being able to react instinctively without premeditated action. The maxim can also be written in the opposite order as *musō-munen*.

Winged monsters of human stature that feature in Japanese folklore. *Tengu* live in the mountains, have both human and bird-like features, are able to fly, posses magical powers, are fiercely proud, and often carry a fan made of leaves or feathers. *Tengu* that resemble humans have red faces and extremely long noses and often wear the robes of *yamabushi* mountain ascetics. Those *tengu* more resembling birds have beaks, claws, and feathers, and are generally crow-like in appearance. *Tengu* were renowned for their prowess in martial arts and many tales exist of humans dueling with *tengu* or receiving combat instruction from them.

Kage means 'shadow' and *musha* means 'warrior'. If directly rendered as 'shadow warrior' one might assume the term is related to *shinobi-no-jutsu*, however *kage-musha* refers to a 'body-double' who impersonates an individual to confuse the enemy. A *kage-musha* may portray an individual of political or military significance to ensure the person's safety should an attempt be made on their life. Alternatively, in the event that someone has been assassinated but courses of events were relying on the continued presence of that individual, a *kage-musha* may be used to fool the enemy that the assassination failed. A ruler weak with sickness or old age may also use a *kage-musha* to strategically project a strong public image.

Tsubame is a 'swallow' and *kaeshi* is to 'switch direction'. In *kenjutsu*, *tsubame-gaeshi* means to quickly reverse the cutting path of the sword back in the opposite direction, reminiscent of the nimble mid-flight manoeuvres of a swallow. A number of variations of the technique exist but their development is originally attributed to the swordsman Sasaki Ganryū, a.k.a. Sasaki Kojirō, who was killed by Miyamoto Musashi in their famed duel in 1612. Hand-to-hand techniques of the same name exist in both judo and shorinji kempo.

Sengoku means 'warring provinces' and *jidai* means 'period'. The *Sengoku-jidai* was a tumultuous period of Japanese history famed for constant conflict and power struggles. It began with the Ōnin War in 1467 intil Oda Nobunaga entered Kyoto in 1568. During the *Sengoku-jidai*, the country was divided into provinces governed by warlords known as *sengoku-daimyō* and Oda Nobunaga unified the provinces prior to the Battle of Sekigahara. The namesake for the *Sengoku-jidai* is the Warring States period (403 BC - 221 BC) of ancient China.

Seppa are the small disk-like spacers fitted between *tsuka* and *tsuba*, and between *tsuba* and *habaki* on Japanese *katana*-style swords. *Tsumaru* is a verb which means to be 'stuck', 'clogged', or 'squeezed'. The expression *seppa-tsumaru* refers to a situation in which you are pushed to the wall, cornered, or under great pressure; the connotation being that you cannot draw your sword freely. Nowadays this expression is often used in work situations when under pressure from deadlines and other such business dealings.

Bibliography

- *Budō no Kotoba - Gendai ni ikasu Shōbu no Tessoku*, PHP Kenkyūsho (ed.), 1987.
- *Bujutsu Jiten (Zusetsu)*, Osano J., Shinkigensha, 2003.
- *Kendō Wa-Ei Jiten*, Zen Nihon Kendō Renmei (ed.), Satō Inshokan Inc., 2000.
- *Kōjien (Daigohan)*, Iwanami Shoten, 2004.
- *Nichijōgo no naka no Budō Kotoba Gogen Jiten*, Katō H. & Nishimura R. (ed.), Tōkyōdō Shuppan, 1995.
- *Nihon Budō Jiten (Zusetsu)*, Sasama Y., Kashiwa-Shobō, 2003.
- *Sengoku Jidai Yōgo Jiten*, Togawa J., Gakushū Kenkyūsha, 2006.

Bushido
as Seen by an Englishman

By Michael Ishimatsu-Prime

In April, 2012, I was asked to write a series of short articles in Japanese for publication in the magazine *Town Mook*. They were published in their *Bushidō and Hagakure* edition, and grouped under the heading of *Bushidō as Seen by an Englishman*. This article is based on them.

"Kendo for Life"

When I knew that I was coming to Japan, I promised myself that I would try to learn a Japanese martial art, and kendo was at the top of the list. I had first seen it in a film called *Black Rain* when I was a high school student. There were no kendo clubs in my hometown, but it was always in the back of my mind.

There were several reasons why I wanted to start a martial art. Japan is famous the world over for its budo, and to come to here and be surrounded by so many and not try one would be a wasted opportunity. I also wanted to be able to make Japanese friends, do something traditional, and keep fit. But the main reason is because I wanted to do something different from the team sports that I had played up until then.

I started kendo soon after arriving in Japan in March, 2003. The following September I joined Shūdōkan Club in Kawasaki, which was very close to where I lived. At one of my first practices there I saw an elderly Japanese man, not only fighting, but controlling and beating men much bigger and younger than himself. When I looked at the club register, I found out that he was a H8-dan instructor, the highest grade now attainable. However, I was stunned to find out that he was 89 years old. I had no idea that an 89-year-old man could move so fast!

This was so very different from the sports that I liked when I was growing up – rugby, cricket, hockey, and most of all, football. In these sports you generally reach your peak in your late-twenties, start a gradual decline, and stop playing in your late-thirties or early forties. However, through living and practising kendo in Japan, I came to understand that kendoka tend to get stronger as they age, and still remain competitive against people a lot younger. At the age people would quit other sports, kendo becomes interesting and more of a mental pursuit than a physical one.

During high school and university, I played hockey regularly and represented my school, university and hometown. I was a fairly good goalkeeper. Football, however, has always been my favourite sport, and after graduating university I joined a local Sunday league football team with a couple of friends. I have never been very good at football, but in the first season I played for Rownhams Football Club, we did the league and cup double.

However, as I was by far the weakest player and made only a few substitute appearances I have never felt that I deserved the medals I received because my contribution to the team was minimal. I wanted to do something that was free from the pressure of being on a team, and where the only pressure was from within – something that would be as much of a mental challenge as a physical one, and something that gave me targets to aim towards. After starting kendo, I found that it had everything I was looking for.

There is one elderly sensei that I regularly train with who is 83 years old, and is certainly not in the best of shape physically. When he is sitting in *seiza* he needs help to stand up. He can barely squat into *sonkyo*. He needs help putting on his *men* and *tare*. However, it is a different story once he is standing with *shinai* in hand and *keiko* begins. I am rarely able to land a strike on him, and I have been knocked down, disarmed and run ragged by him many, many times, as I'm sure I will for years more to come. His 60+ years of experience mean a lot more than my comparative youth and physical condition.

What amazes me about kendo, and inspires me to keep practising is that people in their 70s and 80s, of high and low grades, are still striving to be better in *keiko* than they were the previous time. They approach practice with humility, an open mind and an eagerness to learn. No matter how old or how good you are, the real lesson to be gained from kendo is that there is always room for improvement. This is summed up by the following adage written on my favourite *tenugui* – *Keizoku-wa-chikara-nari* (Perseverance is Strength).

I am 37-years-old now and I hope that I'm still enjoying, learning and getting better at kendo in another 37 years and beyond. Kendo and all other budo, constantly put challenges or barriers in the way of your progress, and what is really important is how you respond to them. When you start to think that you are finally getting to grips with kendo, another barrier appears. This, for me, is the attraction of budo – constant learning and development. What I learn in the dojo, I try to use outside of it.

I cannot envisage my life without kendo now. The same can be said for many of my foreign friends who came to Japan in order to further their study in budo, regardless of which one it is. They all came here with the intention of studying for a few months, or a couple of years, and then returning home, but they have never left. Many of them are now married, are homeowners and have started families and businesses. A large part of the reason why they stay in Japan is because of the attraction of budo.

Kendo, Children and Competition

By Dr. Stephen Robert Nagy, Chinese University of Hong Kong

Preamble

On October 14, 2012, the Hong Kong Kendo Association (HKKA) held its 6th Annual Kendo Competition for Novices, which included both adults and children. The youngest participants included a six-year-old girl and boy, as well as other children aged up to 12. Wearing *bōgu* in a competition for the first time, they at times found it difficult to go into *sonkyo*, or wield the *shinai* because of its length and weight. They were also faced with the challenge of striking, and being struck by another child.

Kendo is a physical activity in which we strike each other with bamboo sticks to cultivate our swordsmanship skills, and ourselves. We also participate in competitions to gauge our level and test our skill. In the process of training and participating in competitions, we have all been hit hard, or in places that are not protected by armour. Sometimes this leaves bruises or sore joints, and in some cases broken bones or other injuries.

Based on some recent experiences in competition, training for tournaments, and being in the dojo, this article will discuss ideas about kendo, kids, competitions and training. Questions to be addressed include when is the best time to start teaching kendo? When should we introduce *bōgu*? When is competition appropriate? What and how should we evaluate children in competition? Lastly, how do we prevent injuries and build the confidence of the youngest of kendo players so that they enjoy kendo and learn its fundamentals?

As kendo teachers, how do we prepare young children to participate in competition?

In my case, my teacher stressed that the safety comes first, have fun, and perform with a strong spirit. That being said, it does not prepare us for the obvious emotional challenge when a child loses in a competition, or possibly worse, when they get hit in an unprotected area. Children do not react to pain in the same way as adults do; they do not have the emotional maturity to understand that the strike was just an accident or just bad luck. Sometimes they can fight through the pain, other times the tears win, and they stop until they can pull themselves together.

In this past competition, we experienced a small child getting hit. It was hard to deal with as not only was the little boy part of the dojo that I train at, he was also my son! Watching from a distance, I knew the strike was an accident, and that it hurt, too. Standing back, I was relieved to watch my fellow dojo members and teacher immediately come to encourage my son to continue. Their encouragement, care and words helped him fight through the pain to finish the bout. They also encouraged him to join the league matches as well, which gave him an opportunity to rebuild the confidence lost in the first match through injury. It is a testimony to the importance of good leadership by teachers and sempai to help children develop kendo confidence through supporting their younger members.

How do we referee a kid's match?

This is a difficult question as it depends on the age of the child, and their development and experience. As we cannot expect them to have the precision and power of a teenager, or an adult, how do we assess kendo principles and the all-important *yūkō-datotsu* (valid strike)?

First, we need to recognise that it is probably unrealistic to expect a perfect *ippon* from children under 10. It becomes even more difficult to raise a red or white flag for a *yūkō-datotsu* when they are fighting someone taller. From experience in refereeing a kids' competition at the Kitamoto Summer Kendo Seminar in 2011, and also in Indonesia and Hong Kong, the consensus among experienced kendo teachers seems to be to focus on the child's spirit, or *kiai*, and give them some leeway with regards to striking accuracy and the *ki-ken-tai-itchi* ideal that we strive for in *keiko* and competition.

We must try to acknowledge kendo's softer principles over its harder ones, i.e., technique. Of course, that does not mean that we should dismiss technical skills; rather, when refereeing children in competition, we should encourage soft principles such as correct *rei*, fighting spirit, *kiai* and enthusiasm for the match. By doing so, we can cultivate confidence in the children, and inculcate the philosophical traditions that are strongly associated with kendo, which differentiate it from other sports. Finally, we can find a way to acknowledge through a prize or medal, growth in kendo and as an individual.

How to referee children fighting against bigger children?

Our natural tendency in this case seems to be to support the smaller child. We somehow think it is harder for the smaller child to win, so we should be more sympathetic toward them. In part, this is true, but it is also unfair and wrong when you think about it from the taller/bigger child's point of view. They have to struggle with a smaller opponent; their striking locations become more limited because of differences in height. This means that they have to be precise. Another factor the taller child needs to consider is the appearance of bullying or taking advantage of the smaller child's undeveloped body. Of course, this may not be intentional but it happens.

The question we need to ask ourselves as *shimpan* is what should we do, and how should we avoid bias? First, we can acknowledge that both the taller and smaller children are differently disadvantaged. Understanding this allows us to be fairer in how we referee the match. Second, we can apply slightly different criteria to our evaluation of what makes a solid *yūkō-datotsu*. The smaller child will inevitably not be able to have the power and precision that an older child has, but if they strike fairly accurately, and with the right intention and strong *kiai*, as judges we should recognise that accomplishment.

In the case of the taller child, a similar rule of thumb should apply but in their case we should have higher expectations of what a *yūkō-datotsu* strike is. Third, we can also consider other attributes of the children such as fighting spirit, posture and *kiai*. In short, a comprehensive approach and a realisation that we are biased in refereeing children can help us make better decisions about children's performances in competitions.

In Hong Kong, we also have the case of older but smaller children who are very accomplished kendo players. At first glance, they appear very young because of their height, but when they enter competitions, one soon realises that their height is not reflective of their age or abilities. In this case what should we do? I would argue that the above case applies. Also, experienced competition organisers would have already tried their best to match up children with similar ages and hopefully levels of experience in order to avoid a very one sided match that would not build confidence or a love for kendo in the younger child.

When to put on bōgu?

I believe that most teachers would agree that it depends on the child, their dexterity, body type and strength. Even children's *bōgu* weighs a lot and considering the average size of a six or seven-year-old, *bōgu* is a heavy burden for their little bodies. This raises interesting questions about modifying *bōgu* so that it is light enough for small children to wear, but strong and robust enough to protect them from injury.

In Shoujinkan, our dojo, we had several six-year-old children that had been practising kendo just in *hakama* and *keiko-gi*, move to wearing *bōgu* at the same time. This was purposeful as it gave them the immediate chance to train in *bōgu* with similarly aged children. It also allowed them to start to train and build confidence with children of similar height and ability. Furthermore, it prevented injuries as the new-comers were not mismatched. Finally, I think introducing them to *bōgu* in a batch allowed the dojo to introduce basic etiquette and *bōgu* wearing principles in a uniformed way.

The role of sempai in the dojo and at competitions

Young children in any activity require care, attention and guidance. Sempai have a very important role here, not only in terms of directions and how to "do" a *shiai*, but also to support the younger members psychologically and physically. When I say physically, we have to keep in mind that using *bōgu* – wearing a *men*, tying one's *tare* – is not easy. Sempai need to watch and be aware how the smaller children are wearing their *bōgu*. Is the *men* too tight or too loose? Are their *hakama* falling down which could lead to them tripping? Is their *dō* hanging too high or too low, preventing them from moving naturally? There are so many things that we need to consider because children have slightly different needs and levels of coordination.

Psychologically, children need lots of encouragement to get through loss or injury that they might incur during training or a match. In the dojo this is easier as it is a familiar setting and the children are surrounded by people they know and trust. This is different in a competition setting. The pressure of competition, large crowds and rules and regulations that the children might not really understand require sempai to provide a more empathetic approach to young children.

Referees can encourage the competing children by ushering them into the right position. They can also spend a little more time explaining *hansoku*. They can talk to the child at eye-level when explaining different aspects of the competition and encouraging them to fight on after an injury. Sempai can also do many things to support the children, including standing nearby the court and explaining that the competition is not just about winning, but is also about having a strong spirit.

Conclusion

There are no perfect answers to the questions raised in this article. That being said, we can share our experiences to ensure that the youngest members of our dojo learn about kendo and participate in competitions safely, happily and in a way that builds confidence, and hopefully a love for kendo. The smiles in the photographs illustrate that sentiment as the success of the youngest members of our dojo also provides older kendo practitioners with the opportunity to pass on their experience and knowledge of kendo, to hone their teaching skills (this does not only include kendo skills), and to develop leadership and teamwork skills as well.

BOOK MARK

KENDO—APPROACHES FOR ALL LEVELS—
Sotaro Honda Kendo Renshi 7-dan

Reviewed by Dr. Sergio Boffa

I first met Honda Sotarō (R7-dan) about ten years ago. Since then, I have been fortunate enough to have enjoyed *keiko* with him on several occasions in either Europe or Japan. The image of his kendo that is etched in my mind is of one that is dynamic and fluid. But what impressed me the most about Honda-sensei was the way he moved his body. He demonstrated clearly, as one of my sensei constantly reminds me, that kendo is not only about rushing forward to the opponent; we should also use lateral movement or *tai-sabaki*.

There is no doubt that Honda-sensei is one of the few sensei who inspire my kendo. However, being an old fashioned scholar, I know that mastering the art of the sword and writing about it are two different exercises, and people who excel in both activities are rare. Let us see if Honda-sensei is able to meet that challenge!

Instead of translating the work of one of his own sensei, why did Honda-sensei choose to add a new title to the already comprehensive collection of books on kendo? What were his objectives? The answer is quite simple. Despite all the qualities that books written by Japanese sensei possess, these books are written for a Japanese readership. Honda-sensei, on the contrary, equipped with extensive experience as a university and national team coach abroad, tried to write a book specifically for non-Japanese kendoka; that is to say, for practitioners that begin kendo at an advanced age and who do not have the opportunity to train every day or meet high-ranking sensei often.

The book itself consists of 13 chapters, and to describe all of them in detail is beyond the scope of this review, especially since they are packed with advice and ideas. Since some parts of this book were previously published in the *British Kendo Association Newsletter* and in *Kendo World*, the

reader can always consult these editions to satisfy their curiosity and discover the inventiveness and the deepness of Honda-sensei's work.

The first chapter, "A Comparison of Circumstance", is especially interesting for those who have not had the chance to visit and train in Japan. The author describes how kendo is practised in Japan, whether in elementary school, high school, university or in local dojo. He then compares this situation with foreign countries, particularly Europe. Such a comparison is rich in teaching and allows the author to conclude:

"It is not always effective for Western kendo practitioners to follow the Japanese process of learning kendo. It would be more suitable for Westerners to modify and devise suitable *keiko* methodology with due consideration to the age of the student and frequency of *keiko* opportunities."

This can be seen as Honda-sensei's main motivation to write his book, as well as being indicative of his own pedagogical approach.

The second and third chapters are devoted to footwork – a fundamental aspect of training for beginners and advanced practitioners alike. The importance of *fumikiri*, *fumikomi* and *hikitsuke* is discussed, together with details on how to integrate them into a correct attack with the help of exercises such as *kūkan-datotsu* and *kihon-uchi*.

The next chapters talks about *kirikaeshi* and *uchikomi-geiko*. Honda-sensei explains his methodology in which cuts evolve from "big, slow and accurate", through "big, quick and accurate", to eventually "small, quick and accurate." He then explains how to make the transition from "big, slow and accurate" to "small, quick and accurate" through the use of different exercises (*waza-geiko*). For this, Honda-sensei suggests three different ways of practicing: "*waza-geiko* for building up *waza*"; "*waza-geiko* for developing and refining *waza*"; "*waza-geiko* for making *waza* practical."

The sixth chapter is devoted to the much maligned *kakari-geiko*. The author stresses the importance of such an exercise, proposes different ways of approaching it, emphasises the ideal behavior of *kakarite* and *motodachi*, and gives some specific advice to foreign practitioners.

Ji-geiko is discussed in two chapters, the first of which highlights the close relationship that exists between *kihon-geiko*, *kata-geiko* and *ji-geiko*. Honda-sensei not only presents different ways to perform *ji-geiko* according to whether we are *kyūsha* or *yūdansha*, but also if our opponent is of a different age, gender or skill level.

Shiai is not forgotten and is the subject of chapters nine and ten. The author focuses heavily on the relative importance of *shiai* in the general practice of kendo. Honda-sensei also pays attention to the proper attitude that must be adopted by competitors, supporters and instructors. This part is one of the too few passages devoted to *reigi*. Finally, he presents various training methods that will be interesting to try in your own dojo.

The final three chapters are devoted to tactics. Honda-sensei does not view tactics as tricks used to easily defeat an opponent or ways in which to circumvent *shiai* rules, but as something that links *kihon-geiko* to *ji-geiko* and *shiai*. Tactics help the kendoka to choose the appropriate technique for any given situation. Again, Honda-sensei proposes different approaches depending on the reader's level.

To conclude, Honda-sensei's work is both well written and easy to understand, and touches of humour and personal anecdotes make the text very enjoyable to read. The book also explains a number of important concepts (*en*, *ki-ken-tai-itchi*, *kime*, etc.), and provides a large number of extremely interesting ideas. Once these are grasped by the practitioner, they will allow them to structure and organise their training, even in the absence of an experienced sensei. This is ideal for most of us that train outside Japan.

It is mentioned earlier that some chapters have been previously published in the British *Kendo Association Newsletter* and *Kendo World*. Some might wonder if they should therefore purchase this book since a great part of it is already available. The answer to this question is an unequivocal "yes"! First, because the new material is extremely interesting, but also because the passages previously published have been rewritten. Finally, the arrangement of the chapters allows the author to develop his methodology in a much more systematic way than what is possible in a series of separate articles.

Is Honda-sensei's book perfect? Probably not, but in view of his motivations and objectives, it is definitely a job well done. Personally, I would not hesitate to say that *Kendo–Approaches for all Levels* is one of the best kendo instruction manuals that I have ever read. I strongly recommend you purchase this book, and more importantly, study it.

Title: Kendo–Approaches for all Levels
Author: Sotaro Honda
Publisher: Bunkasha International Corporation, Tokyo, 2012
Available from Amazon in paperback and Kindle formats.

Hitler's Bogu

By Alex Bennett

It is exquisite. The craftsmanship evident in this extraordinary set of pre-war *bōgu* is nothing short of inspirational. Assembled by craftsmen working for Ōwada Budōgu in Kyoto, the *men* is made from a 1-*bu* 2-*rin* hand stitched *futon*, as is the *tare*, and supposedly the *kote*, which have long been missing. Given that 1-*bu* 5-*rin* was considered to be the finest quality for a set of luxury *bōgu* in its day, the 1.2 stitching represents an absolute labour of love and a piece of awe-inspiring workmanship. It looks as if it could be worn right now to fulfil its curtailed mission to protect the body from *shinai* strikes. You just know that the *futon* would magically mould itself to the wearer's body for a perfect fit.

Then there is the *dō*. It is a *sakura-dō* – a 43-slat bamboo base covered in leather, and then a layer of cherry tree bark. Emblazoned with a subtle Japanese flag in the top left corner, and inscribed with the name of one of history's most infamous villains on the inside, its sublime beauty is contrasted with memories of a dark, militaristic past. The set, now displayed in a glass case in the Budokan office of the All Japan Kendo Federation, is a timeless treasure. Nevertheless, despite representing the highest form of artistry in its construction and appearance, it will be remembered for another, nefarious reason. It was beauty betrothed to the beast – a beast that epitomises pure evil. The *bōgu* was made as a gift to present to Adolf Hitler in 1938.

In November 1936, the "Anti-Comintern Pact" was initiated by Japan and Germany, and joined by their ally Italy a year later. They then signed the "Tripartite Pact" four years later in Berlin on September 27, 1940. The axis of friendship between Japan and these fascist European states was supposedly to counter the Soviet Union and communist influence, but to Japan, it was also a means to expand its imperialist arm throughout the rest of Asia.

One small event in commemoration of the strengthening relations between these countries was the dispatch of Japanese budo students on a tour of cultural exchange and friendship. On March 18, 1938, the Terukuni-maru departed the port of Kobe for Naples. On board was a 15-member student delegation that was comprised of six kendo and six judo exponents and three chaperones. The kendo students were: Kaneko Hiroshi (Tokyo Imperial Univ.); Ōta Shigeru (Keio Univ.) Yuno Masanori (Tokyo Higher Normal School); Hoshino Kōhei (Waseda Univ.); Nishiyama Daisuke (Osaka Univ. of Commerce); and Ishihara Tadayoshi (Budo Vocational School, Busen).

The delegation was aboard the Terukuni-maru for one month, spending their time training on the deck of the ship, before arriving in Naples.

Reaching port on April 18, they then started their tour as ambassadors of friendship through the main cities of Italy and Germany. In Napoli, the students were greeted by members of the Gioventù Italiana del Littorio (GIL) (Italian Youth of the Lictor), youth movement of the National Fascist Party of Italy. The Italian youth demonstrated fencing and wrestling to their Japanese guests who reciprocated with a show of kendo and judo. The kendo demonstration consisted of *kata*, *sanbon-shōbu* matches, *kakari-geiko* and *kirikaeshi*. Apparently the raucous display of frantic attacking by young men dressed in what looked like traditional samurai garb enthralled the Italian hosts.

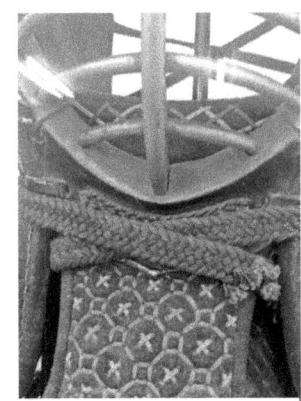

From Naples, the delegation travelled to Rome, Florence, and then Milan. When in Rome on April 27, the delegation met with Benito Mussolini, the leader of the National Fascist Party. After watching an impressive display of Japanese budo, he was presented with a set of kendo equipment which included an extravagant set of *bōgu* crafted by Ōwada Budōgu, a *bokutō*, *shinai*, *keiko-gi* and *hakama*. To my knowledge, the whereabouts of this gift is long unknown.

While the group was in Bologna, they were able to meet Adolf Hitler in person on May 3. Apparently he was there for an emergency meeting with his Italian counterpart. Hitler was not given his *bōgu* at this meeting. Rather, it was presented to him by the Japanese ambassador in Berlin.

From Italy, the delegation then travelled to Germany. They visited Munich on May 14, and once more exhibited their arts to a gathering of 5,000 Germans. Members of the Hitler Youth also performed gymnastics and wrestling in honour of their guests, and as judo had amassed quite a following in Europe by this time, a match between the European champion and a judo student from the Budo Vocational school was held. Managing to preserve the honour of his countrymen, the Busen student won the bout. The delegation also demonstrated in Nuremburg on May 17, and then at the massive Berlin Olympic wresting venue on May 26 in front of many Nazi Party dignitaries. This was the last exhibition, but the group continued their tour of other main centres in Germany, including Dresden and Hamburg, before returning to Japan. The rest is, as they say, history…

Hitler's set of *bōgu* was returned to Japan in 1996. After Berlin collapsed on May 8, 1945, a French officer retrieved the *bōgu* and took it back as a keepsake. From there, the *bōgu* changed hands between collectors, and eventually found its way into the possession of an antiques dealer who just happened to be a former practitioner of kendo. Through this connection, the *bōgu* was purchased by Yoshimura Ken'ichi-sensei (K8-dan), a Japanese man who has spent many years of his life promoting kendo in France. Yoshimura-sensei kindly donated the *bōgu* to the AJKF, and there it remains for all to ponder its beauty and fascinating history.

I know that if it had ended up in my ownership, I would surely have put it on and given it at least one test drive. I wonder if this superb *bōgu* has ever experienced the joy of *keiko*. It seems like such a waste for it to have been a museum-piece all of its life without once absorbing the blow of a *shinai*…

It's ACADEMIC
Notes from THE JAPANESE ACADEMY OF BUDO

In the 1960s, scholars recognised there was a need for sound academic analysis of the technical, historical, cultural and social aspects of budo. The Nippon Budokan led a movement to create an elite academic society dedicated to budo research. The Japanese Academy of Budo (Nihon Budō Gakkai) was officially launched on December 25, 1967. Each year, members congregate for the annual convention to present and discuss all aspects of budo culture. *The Research Journal of Budo* is the society's refereed journal in which scholars can present the findings of their research in the public domain. It is published four times a year with the assistance of the Nippon Budokan. The contents of the journal are now available to members on the "Articles Database" accessible through the academy's homepage. In this section of *Kendo World* we will introduce two or three research abstracts from the plethora of research available. In this issue, we will take a brief look at some of the papers published in 2011. The Japanese Academy of Budo is keen to increase its international membership. Please visit the following homepage: www.budo. ac. It is mainly in Japanese for the moment, but the English content is growing.

(Note: Although the abstracts are published in English, some of the original wording has been modified to suit KW editorial conventions.)

A Study into the Process of Establishment of Kendo in Greece
—From Establishment Up Until the Present Day—

(*Research Journal of Budo* Vol. 43, No. 2, pp. 13–24, 2011)

Nobuyuki ŌNO[1], Sōtarō HONDA[2], Kunihide KŌDA[3], Kengo KUBOTA[4], Yutaka YOSHIMIZU[5]

Abstract

To support the development of kendo in other countries it is important to understand how it is practised, and to examine the future direction of its progression considering the circumstances in each country. This study pays attention to kendo in Greece, and details how the Hellenic Kendo Iaido Naginata Federation (HKINF) was started, and how it has been developed until the present day. The research methods employed were interviews and e-mail correspondence with the staff members of the HKINF and Japanese people living in Greece. Also the "EKF Yudansha List" inside the *EKF Newsletter* published by the European Kendo Federation (EKF) was referred to.

In 1997, Mr. Ioannis Papadimitriou started the process to establish the HKINF. The federation was properly established in 1999. The HKINF was officially recognised by the EKF in 2000 and the International Kendo Federation in 2006.

In the HKINF there are six affiliated clubs. The number of registered members is 122; among those 32 hold *dan* grades. Three kendo tournaments are held every year in Greece: "The All Greek Kendo Championships", "Combat Sport Tournament Ioannou Eleni" and "Thessaloniki Kendo Cup". The Greek National Kendo Team has taken part in the European Kendo Championships and the World Kendo Championships. They have also participated in the "Balkan Kendo Cup" and competitions around the Balkan Peninsula area.

One of the goals of the HKINF is to encourage the development of coaching and refereeing. Another goal is to try to keep people interested in kendo. To do this, the HKINF needs to take positive action to improve their own management skills, and to nurture teachers and referees in the future.

---

1) Kurume University, Institute of Health and Sports
2) Fukuoka University of Education
3) Tsukuba University
4) Sasaguri Primary School
5) Kurume University

A Study about the Symbol Geom "剑" in Korean Martial Arts Books of the Choson Yi Dynasty

(*Research Journal of Budo* Vol. 44, No. 2, pp. 65–81, 2011)

Junko ŌISHI [1)2)], Toshinobu SAKAI [3)], Guoeng QU [4)]

Abstract

The purpose of this study is to research usage of the symbol for *geom* (剑=sword) in Korean martial art texts written in the Choson Yi dynasty, and to discuss the background surrounding its usage in Korea. There are two types of symbols to describe swords: One of them is *geom* (剑) which means double-edged sword. The other is *do* (刀) which refers to swords with a single edge. The conclusions of this study are as follows:

1. Some techniques for single-edged swords mentioned in Korean martial arts books originated in the text *Ji-Xiao-Xin-Shu* (紀效新書) written in Ming dynasty China. To describe the techniques of swords with a single cutting edge, the character for *do* (刀) was used in the *Ji-Xiao-Xin-Shu*; however, similar techniques were described with the symbol of *geom* in some other Korean martial arts texts. The *Ji-Xiao-Xin-Shu* was also published in the Choson Yi dynasty, at which time the techniques for single-edged swords were also described with the symbol for *geom*.

2. The *Mye-jebo* (武芸諸譜) is a Korean martial art text. The usage *geom* in the *Mye-jebo* influenced usage of the character in other Korean martial arts texts.

3. The usage of the symbol for *geom* was found in some books about Korean court rituals that were written in the middle of the fifteenth century.

4. Single-edged swords called *geom* were worn in early Korean court rituals. We think the custom influenced the usage of the character for *geom* in Korean martial arts texts.

5. We also contend that some of the traditional ideals related to *geom* in Tang, Sung China, and ancient Korea influenced the usage of the kanji for *geom* in later Korean martial arts books.

---

1) Yashima Gakuen University
2) Graduate School of Comprehensive Human Sciences, Doctoral Program in Physical Education, Health and Sport Sciences, University of Tsukuba
3) Comprehensive Human Sciences, University of Tsukuba
4) Beijing Normal University

ADVERTISEMENT

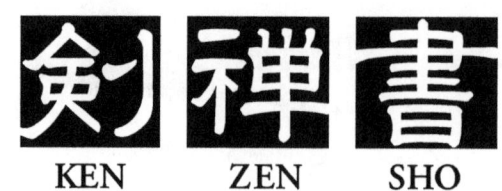

KEN ZEN SHO

THE ZEN CALLIGRAPHY AND PAINTING OF YAMAOKA TESSHŪ

Yamaoka Tesshū (1836-1888) was a Japanese master of the sword, Zen and calligraphy. This full-color book on the Zen art of Yamaoka Tesshū features reproductions of extremely valuable calligraphy pieces, and also a number of essays about the relationship between swordsmanship, the study of Zen, and calligraphy. All of the works presented are translated into English, and its significance explained in detailed captions. Some fantastic specimens of Zen calligraphy by Tesshū's famous contemporaries Katsu Kaishū and Takahashi Deishū (Tesshū's brother-in-law), and modern master Terayama Tanchū are also featured.

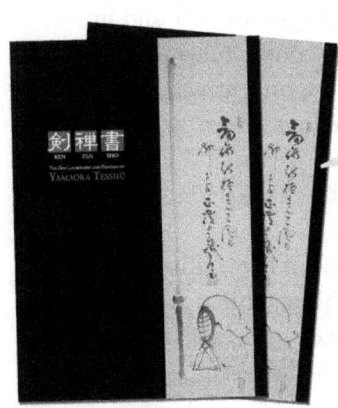

Size: A4 Colour/Black&White
ONLINE STORE PRICE IS
US $ 64.95
+ SHIPPING & HANDLING

Yamaoka Tesshū (1836–1888)
Dragon (cursive script) 1885.
Sumi ink on paper 130cm × 56cm.

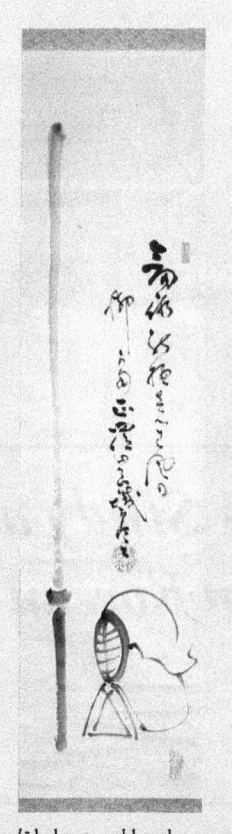

Kendō helmet and bamboo sword
(with inscription in cursive script) 1886.
Sumi ink on paper 130cm × 30cm.

Katsu Kaishū (1823-1899)
Pine (with inscription in cursive script) 1895. *Sumi* ink on paper 134cm × 53cm.

Takahashi Deishū (1835–1903)
One line saying (cursive script) 1900. *Sumi* ink on paper 134cm × 64cm.

Terayama Tanchū (1938–2007)
One line saying (cursive script) Autumn 2004. *Sumi* ink on paper 164cm × 33cm.

To order, visit **www.kendo-world.com** more information, mail to **info@kendo-world.com**

Published by **BUNKASHA** INTERNATIONAL CORPORATION / Suga 488-1-501, Onjuku, Chiba, Japan 299-5106

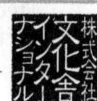

The Development of Kendo in Slovenia

By Peter Topić, Kendo 4-dan (President of the Kendo Federation of Slovenia)
Photographs by Grega Žunič

Slovenia, a small European country with a population of only two million people, is situated between the Alps and the Mediterranean Sea. Strange as it may seem, in a country this small, one can find a couple of dojo where you can practice kendo, and you are most welcome to do so. In this article, I would like to introduce the origins and continued growth of kendo in Slovenia.

Kendo does not have a long tradition in Slovenia, as opposed to other European countries like Italy, France, Belgium, England, Germany and Hungary, and it is not surprising that the kendo community in those countries is far bigger. Martial arts like karate, aikido and judo have a much longer tradition in Slovenia, and are far more popular and commercialised.

Beginning in 1985, there have been several attempts to introduce kendo to Slovenia, but real progress started in 1999 when two kendoka formed their own dojo in two different towns: Iss-Hogai in Velenje, and Shidokai in Kranj. This led to kendo practice starting on a regular basis and the formation of the Kendo Federation of Slovenia (KFSLO) the following year. In the same year, the KFSLO organised the National Championships and several tournaments at Iss-Hogai and Shidokai. There were also many activities that included kendo demonstrations in order to popularise kendo in Slovenia. In April 2001, the European Kendo Championship (EKC) was held in Italy, during which the KFSLO became a member of the European Kendo Federation.

An important milestone for Slovenian kendo was the participation of two Slovenian kendoka at the 1st Kendo Summer Seminar in Copenhagen, Denmark, in August 2002. The seminar was organised by the Danish Kendo Federation, in cooperation with the All Belgium Kendo Federation (ABKF),

The Development of Kendo in Slovenia

Hirakawa-sensei

and was conducted by Hirakawa Nobuo-sensei (Kendo K8-dan, Iaido K7-dan). At that seminar, the two participating KFSLO members asked Hirakawa-sensei and representatives of the ABKF for any kind of support which would help develop kendo in Slovenia. Upon returning home, those two members then organised a seminar at which they presented the valuable knowledge gained at the Danish seminar. Also, there was a discussion on the future course of kendo in Slovenia.

The beginnings of kendo in Slovenia were not easy for those pioneers, but they possessed an incredible zeal to acquire any kind of information to improve their kendo, and popularise it in Slovenia. It took a lot of travelling around Europe, which posed a great financial burden as there was virtually no support from any institution, and the few enthusiasts were left more or less to their own devices.

In December 2002, three members of Slovenian dojo took part in the 11th Winter Seminar and Nakakura Cup, organised by the ABKF, in Brussels. At the seminar, there were around 200 participants from Holland, Sweden, Finland, France, Germany Italy, England, Poland, Turkey, Denmark, Belgium and Slovenia. The seminar was conducted by a 22-strong Japanese delegation led by Hirakawa-sensei. Participation in this important event was another step in the right direction for the growth and improvement of kendo in Slovenia.

In 2003, two Slovenians participated in the Kendo Summer Seminar in Belgium. On the final day of the seminar, both passed the examinations for 1-*kyu* and *shodan*, the first internationally recognised kendo *dan* grade in Slovenia. It was confirmation that we had set upon the right path, following the guidelines laid out by Hirakawa-sensei. The seminar was also an occasion to invite him to visit Slovenia.

It is hard for a *shodan* to run a dojo. Despite this, some people were willing to drive by car for almost two hours five times a week to practise for an hour and a half. They did just that for more than a year to learn kendo and grab any piece of newly gained knowledge brought from abroad. I believe that this kind of dedication and hard training is instrumental in moving people to a higher level.

In August 2003, the KFSLO organised the 1st International Kendo Seminar in Slovenia, which brought together 33 kendoka from Belgium, Croatia, Slovenia and other members of the former republics of Yugoslavia. The KFSLO organised the event in cooperation with the ABKF. In 2010, almost seven years later, the 2nd kendo seminar and the 1st Samurai Cup were held in Slovenia. The seminar attracted more than 100 kendoka

2012 seminar participants

from Austria, Belgium, Bulgaria, Croatia, Hungary, Italy, Israel, Montenegro, Poland, Romania, Russia, Serbia, Switzerland, and Slovenia and it turned out to be a great success. The seminar was conducted in cooperation with the ABKF and was conducted by Hirakawa-sensei, who was accompanied by four high-ranked Japanese sensei and two high-ranked European sensei. It was a four-day seminar held in the Slovenian capital of Ljubljana. We also held a summer seminar in 2011 and 2012 and we are planning to organise another one in 2013. All the aforementioned seminars were attended by more than 100 kendoka and were conducted by Hirakawa-sensei.

At the last seminar held in Ljubljana in the summer of 2012, we were honoured to have been visited by seven high ranked Japanese sensei as well as some high ranked European teachers from Belgium, Italy and France. Kendoka from Austria, Belgium, Bulgaria, Brazil, Croatia, France, Germany, Israel, Italy, Japan, Switzerland and Slovenia participated in the four-day seminar, and they were also able to grade up to 5-dan.

The seminars are led by Hirakawa-sensei whose instruction is always very interesting because he emphasises the connection between the cuts that we do with a *shinai*, with those of a *katana*. One of the most interesting things was *happō-giri*, which includes eight directions of cutting using *shinai*. For kendoka who do not practice iaido, this teaches the various *hasuji* that are not seen in regular kendo. We also practiced *katate-waza*, which are very hard and complicated at first, but help to develop a flexible wrist for correct *tenouchi* later on when using both hands. The hallmarks of Hirakawa-sensei's teachings are a focus on correct *shisei* (posture) and *seme* during practice. He always teaches us that while practising kendo, one always needs a straight heart and a replete spirit, never looking for a shortcut just to get an *ippon*.

Most of the seminars are concluded with a *shiai*, the Samurai Cup. All the matches are *ippon-shōbu*, which presents the practitioners with the reality of a very narrow margin of error. In 2011, we were proud that the Samurai Cup was won by a Slovenian kendoka, but this year's champion was a Belgian. Slovenian practitioners still often have to travel long distances to practice and take part in competitions abroad, but it is also important to have events like the seminar and Samurai Cup organised in our country, too.

At present, Slovenia has 50 members who have participated at numerous seminars and competitions all around Europe. Currently, there are five clubs in the KFSLO, the latest, the Club of Japanese Swordsmanship in Maribor, joined at the beginning of 2012. Without a permanent high ranked teacher in Slovenia, the members are trying their best to educate themselves abroad, attending seminars and joining *keiko* with the clubs in nearby countries such as Austria, Croatia, Italy, etc. Considering the young age of the KFSLO, Slovenian kendoka have made remarkable progress over the past ten years, which can be seen by a constant advance in *dan* gradings as well as by their achievements in international competitions. Slovenia participated in the EKC in 2004, 2008 and 2010. We have also participated in *shimpan* seminars in Austria and Belgium to gain knowledge and bring it to Slovenia.

At the time I started practising kendo in 2003,

The Development of Kendo in Slovenia

it was in a very small gym in Kranj that only a few people regularly attended. There was little knowledge and no *dan* level practitioners in Slovenia. To practice when you feel that there is not enough structure and security behind your efforts is hard, as it is to build certainty and self-confidence. We are at the point now where four Slovenian practitioners have been awarded 4-dan, and several others have attained other *dan* grades.

In the beginning, we practised the Nippon Kendo Kata a lot, but there was almost no explanation of the psychology and reason behind it. Meeting a real sensei in Brussels for the first time was a blessing and a relief. I have great respect for those people who started studying kendo in Slovenia, but when I met Hirakawa-sensei for the first time, I saw someone with a level high enough to teach the philosophy behind the practice of budo, especially kendo, and the *riai* (principles) of the Nippon Kendo Kata. Listening to and watching an 8-dan explaining and showing you something is very different from reading a book or watching a video about it.

When I started practising kendo at the age of 40, I was desperate to find some peace of mind. However, not knowing and understanding the reason of doing something left me feeling empty and uncertain. I did not want my kendo practice to become merely an aerobic activity or sport. It is not so paradoxical to choose martial arts when trying to find peace of mind. If we take into consideration the "Concept of Kendo" and the "Purpose of Practicing Kendo", we find many answers to our questions: developing mind, body and spirit; correct training; striving for improvement; human courtesy and honour; sincerity; and an on-going pursuit of the cultivation of the self. Furthermore, kendo and its etiquette seemed the right way for me to do this. When I began to figure out the *riai*, it had a profound effect on my understanding of kendo and how I viewed myself and the world around me.

Many people in our culture show great interest in Japan, its culture and its martial arts. My experience is that all events presenting Japanese culture or martial arts in Slovenia are always well attended. Even more interestingly, the young generation is attracted to different Japanese martial arts. They are fascinated by stories of samurai and bushido. There are several books about these topics translated into Slovenian, and Nitobe Inazo's *Bushido* is one that was published in Slovenia last year. It seems that, despite different cultural and religious backgrounds, people from all around the world are drawn to the same universal principles and to the way of the warrior.

I believe that in order to understand how to discipline the human character through the application of the "principles of the *katana*", it is

necessary to study Japanese culture and the way of Japanese warriors of old. Hopefully, there is a very slim chance that a kendoka will be faced with a life threatening situation in which they will need to, or even be able to use a sword, but there are countless situations every day where all of us need to control ourselves. It is important that people who start practising kendo also learn about its origins, and think about the reasons why they do it.

At the last seminar held in Ljubljana, Hirakawa-sensei expressed beautifully the wisdom of Shimada Toranosuke: "If you want to study the sword, you have to study the heart." I strongly believe that the values a person can gain through dedicated kendo practice are as important, or even more important, in today's fast changing world as they were in the past. If we compare the purpose of practising kendo with a contemporary book on neuroscience, we can easily find more similarities than differences when it comes to discipline, developing the mind and moulding the human character. The first one is ancient wisdom, and the second is contemporary science, but both teach the same principles.

This is an important observation necessary to be incorporated into planning future strategies of presenting kendo to the general public in Slovenia. It includes writing articles, filming documentaries, making short videos to post on the internet, and planning demonstrations of kendo in schools. I believe that the young generation today is even more in need of the qualities and values that kendo has to offer.

A goal of the KFSLO is to participate in the EKC and the World Kendo Championship, and also to become a member of the International Kendo Federation. Within the next five years, the KFSLO would like to accomplish the goal of making kendo attractive and available to children in Slovenia. For this to become reality, we need to have a team of teachers who are willing and skilled enough to work with the next generation of practitioners, who will in turn cultivate and practice this important martial art and present it to future generations.

At this point I wish to thank the All Japan Kendo Federation and its representatives, for all the help we have received from them in the past years. We hope that our future efforts will be noticed by the people who have the power to make our path easier to travel.

The author with Hirakawa-sensei

The Dai Nippon Butokukai Naginatadō Kihon Dōsa
薙刀道基本動作

By Baptiste Tavernier

Introduction

In 1941 the Dai Nippon Butokukai published a set of generic *kata* and teaching guidelines entitled *Naginatadō Kihon Dōsa,* for the purpose of promoting a unified form of naginata in schools, as it had already been the case with kendo in 1906 (Dai-Nippon Butokukai Seitei Kenjutsu Kata - for more information refer to *Kendo World 5.2*, pp. 29-38).

Naginata was admitted in girls schools since 1913 as an extracurricular activity and was furthemore elevated to an elective subject from 1937. However, naginata instruction in schools had always consisted in the study of *ryūha* techniques, mainly from the Tendō-ryū and the Jikishin Kage-ryū traditions (also rarely from a few more 'minor' *ryūha* such as the Kyōshin-ryū or the Bukō-ryū). Thus, and contrary to kendo which had a somehow unified curriculum since the Taishō period, naginata instruction was totally different from one school to the other, depending on which *ryūha* was traditionally taught in the area. That was indeed a barrier to naginata dissemination nationwide, and therefore the Butokukai decided to address the matter.

The now infamous *Shin Budō* ("New Budo"), a militarist and nationalist magazine published during the war, rejoices in its 1941/05 issue (*cf.* p. 68):

"Naginata moves and styles vary from one tradition to the other and as a result, this was a cause of worries for the promotion of naginata in schools. There has been for a long time a hope for a unified style; at last, the Butokukai has just created the *Naginata Kihon Dōsa*. This long pending problem has finally been solved. This should be congratulated."

The *Dai-Nippon Butokukai Naginatadō Kihon Dōsa Guidelines* provide a unified form of *reihō* (etiquette), *kamae*, footwork, *zangeki* (cuts) and a set of 5 *kata* that would be later known as "Butokukai Seitei Kata". The original textbook does not feature any illustrations. However, the guidelines have been fortunately quoted or republished several times during the war in a fistful of manuals that contain pictures or drawings of the *kata*.

Naginatadō Kihon Dōsa starts with a short foreword and a general introduction:

"The Dai-Nippon Butokukai recognises the value of *naginata-jutsu* as a form of budo for girls. We opened a *naginata-jutsu* training course at our Head Quarters and we have been trying to promote the art since. We soon came to realise the necessity of raising good instructors and thus founded the Naginata-jutsu Kyōin Yōsei-jo

(Naginata-jutsu Instructor Training Center) in June 1934. Now, we have more than a hundred graduates. [...] We are truly joyful to see how *naginata-jutsu* has become very important as teaching material for physical discipline classes in National People's Schools. [...] Since ancient times, *naginata-jutsu* was studied in various *ryūha* which featured different kinds of *naginata*, ways of handling them, and etiquette. It is thus very difficult to adapt *naginata-jutsu* into a teaching material for schools."

A research committee was appointed by the Butokukai to work on the inception of a unified form of naginata. Members of the committee were:
- **Kendo Hanshi:** Ogawa Kinnosuke and Sonobe Masatoshi.
- **Naginata-jutsu Hanshi:** Sonobe Hideo, Mitamura Chiyo and Yoshimura Seki.
- **Kendo Kyōshi:** Mitamura Kunihiko.
- **Naginatajutsu Kyōshi:** Sonobe Shigehachi, Nishigeki Kin, Sonobe Asano, and Moriya Kuno.
- Seven Butokukai officials and directors were also members of the committee, among them: Mori Hisashi, principal of the Budō Semmon Gakkō, and Konishi Shin'emon, kendo Kyōshi. The following quoted text outlines the process involved in researching new forms of naginata-jutsu for girls' education.

"Committee members are authorities from both the Tendō-ryū and the Jikishin Kage-ryū traditions. The Dai-Nippon Butokukai nevertheless asked each of its regional branches if they knew any naginata *ryūha* with ancient and honourable lineage; research revealed, among others:
- The Suzuka-ryū and the Anasawa-ryū in Miyagi.
- The Jōzan-ryū in Fukushima.
- The Shinkage Hikita-ryū in Tottori.
- The Ōishi Shinkage-ryū in Yamaguchi.
- The Higo-koryū in Kumamoto.

However, as these traditions have a small number of adherents, Tendō-ryū and Jikishin Kage-ryū were both confirmed as the main *ryūha* in *naginata-jutsu*. This is why their representatives were appointed as committee members.

The first research committee meeting was convened on February 27, 1940. Sonobe Masatoshi Hanshi who expressed his deep enthusiasm regarding the committee, regrettably succumbed to an illness a few days before the meeting. A second meeting was held on May 8, a third on September 12, a fourth on October 5-6, and the final one on December 23, 1940. After careful deliberation, we agreed on the guidelines and submitted the final draft to the Budō Kōsa Iinkai [Budo Examination Committee]. The guidelines were adopted at the General Meeting on January 21, 1941."

Reception

The "Dai-Nippon Butokukai Naginata-dō Kihon Dōsa" was received with lukewarm enthusiasm. Shortly after the inception and the publication of the guidelines, Mitamura Chiyo, head of the Tendō-ryū tradition, declared that the *kata* were unrealistic, and she subsequently resigned from her position as Butokukai instructor in May 1941. In the aforementioned *Shin Budō* lampoon (*idem*, p. 68), the incident was depicted as follows:

"There are rumours of some dissatisfaction in some *ryūha* regarding the creation of this unified form of naginata. This is unbelievable! With today's situation, when it comes to budo development each *ryūha* cannot be stubborn about its own principles. Apparently, some people say that one year of discussion and examination was not enough to expound their theories, and that they are not happy with the conclusions... Nothing in budo can be deemed unsuitable. The dissemination of this kind of exaggerated rumour may cause distrust towards the budo world. It comes from overemphasised legends about *ryūha* antagonism and factional disputes. To what extent this kind of gossip can hurt and warp the world of budo? No one can know. People who convey such rumours should endeavour to grasp the whole situation and think first about the good of the budo world."

A closer look at the *kata* will help the reader decide whether or not they were unrealistic; but we can assume in any case that Mitamura Chiyo was displeased not only with the *kata*, but with the fact that most of the techniques were incorporated from the Jikishin Kage-ryū tradition. The five *kamae* follow the Jikishin Kage-ryū style; there is a strong emphasis on *furiage-waza*, and above all on *kuruma-gaeshi waza*, which are "trademark" techniques of this tradition. The only technique in the *kata* that can be identified as a peculiar to Tendō-ryū *waza* would be the first move in *nihon-me*, close to the *harai-otoshi* that can be found in the *kata* named "Tani-tobi".

As a result, the intended unification did not happen and the situation in schools remained unchanged: classes instructed by a Jikishin Kage-ryū instructor were based on the Butokukai's *Naginatadō Kihon Dōsa*, and schools with a Tendō-ryū instructor continued practicing the *kata* of that tradition. Schools where naginata classes were instructed by teachers from neither the Jikishin Kage-ryū nor the Tendō-ryū sometimes adopted the Butokukai's guidelines, and sometimes rejected them choosing instead *kata* or techniques from other traditions, such as the Katori Shintō-ryū.

The *Naginatadō Kihon Dōsa* failed to achieve its purpose because it was seen as a simplification of the Jikishin Kage-ryū more than a unification of different traditions. A few naginata manuals for schools were published by Tendō-ryū exponents during the war (*Gakkō Naginata-dō no Shiori* and *Gakkō Naginata-dō Shūtoku no Shiori* - reprinted in *Kindai Naginata Meicho Senshu 6*); they do not mention the *Naginata-dō Kihon Dōsa* and focus on the Tendō-ryū's standard curriculum. They also surprisingly introduce the "Dai-Nippon Butokukai Shin Seitei Kata" ("Butokukai New Kata") which is a modified version of the previously devised *kata*: it follows the exact same sequence but has the Jikishin Kage-ryū peculiar components expurgated (mainly, *kuruma-gaeshi* strikes are replaced with strikes from *hassō*). On the contrary, the Jikishin Kage-ryū adherents have preserved the *kata* of the *Naginata-dō Kihon Dōsa*, and continued to provide instruction for many years after the war, as one can see in a 1981 book entitled *Zukai Kōchi Naginata*.

The *Naginata-dō Kihon Dōsa* was also a failure in the sense that it did not constitute a modern system where a *naginata* would face another *naginata*. Instead, it still promoted the old pattern of a *naginata* facing a sword, which is inconvenient as a school teaching material because the children have to become 'proficient' in the use of two very different weapons in a short period of time. *Naginata* versus *naginata* methods were to be devised later on by Niino Kyūhei (*Nihon Kokumin Naginata-dō Kyōhon*) and subsequently by Sakakida Yaeko who created a set of techniques that would be later known as the Shikake-ōji and are practised widely today.

Overview of the Guidelines

1. Objectives
"The purpose of this method is to make the basics of *naginata-jutsu* and the *kata* easy to learn, to forge the body and the mind, to cultivate the spirit of budo and to foster womanly virtues.

One shall train with unified mind and body, revere etiquette, embody a sense of honour and cultivate a serene yet resolute character."

2. Equipment
The *naginata* described in the *Naginata-dō Kihon Dōsa* is shorter than the ones used by practitioners of the Jikishin Kage-ryū or Tendō-ryū, evidently because they were to be wielded by children. The guidelines indicate:

"The length of the shaft shall be chosen freely, as long as the total length of the weapon is comprised between 165cm and 180cm."

The guidelines are then divided in 4 parts: *kihon-dōsa*, *oyō-dōsa*, *kata*, and notes for instructors.

3. Kihon-dōsa (Basic movements)
a) Lining up (the heads are facing sideways; on command, heads face forward).

b) Taking position

c) Etiquette
 °*Saikei-rei* (deep bow).
 °*Kei-rei* (standard bow: 30°).
 °*Orishiki* (crouching bow).

d) Kamae
 °*Chūdan* (the *kissaki* is pointing towards the opponent's right eye).
 °*Hassō*.
 °*Jōdan* (the *kissaki* is not on the centreline, but out to the right).
 °*Gedan*.
 °*Waki* (the *ishizuki* is higher than the *kissaki*, and the blade faces diagonally upwards).

e) Footwork
 °*Suri-ashi mae / ato*.
 °*Hiraki-ashi migi / hidari*.
Note: there is no mention of *ayumi-ashi*.

f) Cuts (the term *zangeki* "cut" is used instead of *uchi* "strike")
 °*Furiage* cuts.
 °*Kuruma-gaeshi ue* cuts (this does not exist in modern naginata anymore. It is based on the Jikishin Kage-ryū *waza* called *mizu-guruma*, a kind of inverted *furikaeshi*.
 °*Kuruma-gaeshi shita* cuts (*furikaeshi* in modern naginata).
 °*Tsuki* (*tsuki* from *chūdan* and *furikomi-tsuki*).

g) Targets.
Targets and the cuts that one can use to strike at them:
 °*Shōmen* --> *furiage* ; *kuruma-gaeshi shita*.
 °*Sayūmen* --> *furiage* ; *kuruma-gaeshi ue*.
 °*Sune* --> *furiage* ; *kuruma-gaeshi ue*.

°*Dō --> furiage* ; *kuruma-gaeshi ue.*
°*Kote --> furiage* ; *kuruma-gaeshi ue* ; *kuruma-gaeshi shita.*
°*Inkō tsuki* (thrust to the throat) ; *shinka tsuki* (thrust to the solar plexus).

h) Cuts
This section describes each cut in more detail, with different rhythms (i.e. each cut can be made in one move, two moves, *etc.*)

4. Oyō-Dōsa (Applied movements)
°Nidan-uchi
°Sandan-uchi
°Uchikomi-kirikaeshi

This section does not give any information on the content of each exercise, only the names.

5. Kata
As mentioned in the introduction, the original textbook published by the Butokukai does not feature any illustrations. Fortunately, the guidelines were republished in July 1941 in the book *Kokumin Gakkō Naginata-dō Kyōzai Kaisetsu*. Each *kata* is supplemented with one picture in which represents each step of the sequence. Those pictures are virtually illegible, and we decided not to include them in this article.

In Sonobe Shigehachi's *Naginata Yōgi*, published in 1944, the Butokukai Seitei Kata is supplemented with 24 pictures that illustrate each sequence step by step. However again, the poor quality of the pictures combined with the poor condition of the damaged copy in our possession prevented us for using them in this article. Fortunately, the book *Zukai Kōchi Naginata*, published in 1981, features a new set of 24 illustrations in the exact same positions that were represented in the 1944 book. We thus chose those pictures to illustrate the "Butokukai Seitei Kata" in this article.

Butokukai Seitei Kata: Ippon-me.
Illustration from *Kokumin Gakkō Naginatadō Kyōzai Kaisetsu*

The *kata* guidelines start with an introduction explaining that the *tachi* should be handled the same as in the "Kendō Kihon" and the "Teikoku Kendō Kata" (known nowadays as the Nippon Kendo Kata). There is then an explanation about the different bows, especially the *orishiki* or "crouching bow" for the *tachi* (which is different from the usual *sonkyō*); followed by an explanation about the *reihō* that one must demonstrate between each *kata* and at the end of the whole set.

6. Notes for Instructors
- In every situation, always impart *reihō* to the students.
- Repeat ceaselessly the exercises. Build the students' mental strength.
- Make the students strike at the void before striking at the dummy.
- Always do warm up exercises.
- Make sure that the students understand the principles behind the *kata*.
- Make the students repeat the *kata* alone, then with a partner.
- Make the students recite the written works of the Emperor. Make the students sing the Budo Anthem.
- Balance your classes with both practical training and lectures.
- Follow and respect the sequences prescribed in these guidelines.

References:
°An., "Gakkō Naginatadō no Shiori", in *Kindai Naginata Meicho Senshu 6*, Tokyo, Hon no Yusha, 2004.
°An., "Gakkō Naginatadō Shūtoku no Shiori", in *Kindai Naginata Meicho Senshu 6*, Tokyo, Hon no Yusha, 2004.
°Bennett Alexander, *Naginata: The definitive guide*, Auckland, Kendo World Publication, 2005.
°Dai Nippon Butokukai, *Naginatadō Kihon Dōsa*, Kyoto, Maruyama Kigen, 1941.
°Nakamura Tamio, "Kindai Naginata Shōshi", in *Kindai Naginata Meicho Senshu 8*, Tokyo, Hon no Yusha, 2004.
°Niino Kyūhei, *Nihon Kokumin Naginatadō Kyōhon*, Kyoto, Shinnō-sha, 1941.
°*Shin Budō*, issue 05-1941.
°Shūtokukan Kenkyūbu, *Kokumin Gakkō Naginatadō Kyōzai Kaisetsu*, Tokyo, Shūtokukan Kenkyūbu, 1941.
°Sonobe Shigehachi, *Jōshi Budō Naginata no Tsukaikata*, Tokyo, Tōyō Tosho, 1942.
°Sonobe Shigehachi, *Kokumin Gakkō Naginata Seigi*, Tokyo, Tōyō Tosho, 1941.
°Sonobe Shigehachi, *Naginata Yōgi*, Tokyo, Hōbunkan, 1944.
°Sonobe Shigehachi, *Zukai Kōchi Naginata*, Tokyo, Sebidō Shuppan, 1981.
°Sugino Yoshio, *Naginata Kyōiku no Riron to Jissai*, Tokyo, Kanda Shobō, 1942.

Naginatadō Kihon Dōsa (Butokukai Seitei Kata)

At the beginning of each *kata*, *shidachi* (*naginata*) and *uketachi* (*tachi*) should start from *chūdan*, and then assume the designated *kamae*. At the end of each *kata*, both should first assume *chūdan* again, then go back to the original position assuming *migi-kowaki* (*mugamae* in modern naginata) for *shidachi* and lowering the *kensen* for *uketachi*.

IPPON-ME - JODAN

(1) SHIDACHI: assume *jōdan*, from the back foot take two steps forward into the correct *maai*.

(1) UKETACHI: assume *chūdan* and from the front foot take three steps forward.

(2) SHIDACHI: step forward with the right foot and strike *shōmen*.

(2) UKETACHI: take one step back from the left foot and block the *shōmen* strike.

(3) SHIDACHI: step forward from the left foot and strike *sune* in the *kuruma-gaeshi ue* fashion.

(3) UKETACHI: withdraw the right foot and block the *sune* strike.

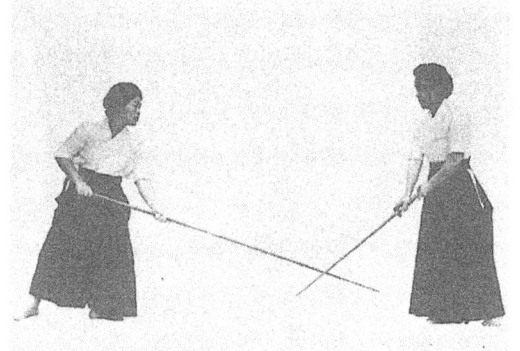

(4) SHIDACHI: step forward from the left foot and thrust to the solar plexus.

(4) UKETACHI: take a step back from the left foot.

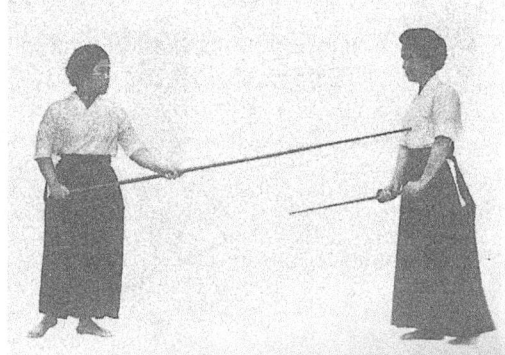

Note: there is one additional picture showing both practitioners standing in shizentai. We chose not to include it here.

NIHON-ME - CHUDAN

(1) SHIDACHI: assume *chūdan*, take two steps forward and take the *maai*.

(1) UKETACHI: assume *hassō* and take three steps forward.

(2) SHIDACHI: step forward with the right foot and keep the legs crossed while blocking in *kasumi-jōdan uketachi*'s *shōmen* strike.

(2) UKETACHI: strike *shōmen*.

(3) SHIDACHI: perform *harai-otoshi* to the right on the *tachi*.

(3) UKETACHI: receive the *harai-otoshi* on your left.

(4) SHIDACHI: step forward with the left foot and thrust to the right flank.

(4) UKETACHI: take a step back from the left foot.

SANBON-ME - GEDAN

(1) SHIDACHI: assume *gedan*, take two steps forward and take the *maai*.

(1) UKETACHI: assume *jōdan* and take three steps forward.

(2) SHIDACHI: step forward from the left foot and strike the *kote* from below.

(2) UKETACHI: withdraw the body and block the ascending *kote* strike.

(3) SHIDACHI: step forward with the right foot and strike *hidari men* in the *kuruma-gaeshi ue* fashion.

(3) UKETACHI: withdraw the left foot and block the *hidari men* strike.

(4) SHIDACHI: step forward from the left foot and with the shaft strike the *migi kote* from below.

(4) UKETACHI: withdraw with the right foot and assume *jōdan*.

YONHON-ME - HASSO

(1) SHIDACHI: assume *hassō*, take two steps forward and take the *maai*.

(1) UKETACHI: assume *hassō* and take three steps forward.

(2) SHIDACHI: step forward with the right foot and strike *hidari-men*.

(2) UKETACHI: withdraw the left foot and block the *hidari men* strike.

(3) SHIDACHI: step forward with the left foot and strike *sune* in the *kuruma-gaeshi ue* fashion.

(3) UKETACHI: withdraw the right foot and block the *sune* strike.

(4) SHIDACHI: step backward with the left foot and "scoop" the *dō* in the *kuruma-gaeshi ue* fashion.

(4) UKETACHI: step forward from the left foot and assume *jōdan*.

GOHON-ME - WAKI

(1) SHIDACHI: assume *migi-waki*, take two steps forward and take the *maai*.

(1) UKETACHI: assume *jōdan* and take three steps forward.

(2) SHIDACHI: step forward with the right foot and strike *dō*.

(2) UKETACHI: withdraw the left foot and block the *dō* strike.

(3) SHIDACHI: step forward with the left foot and strike *sune* in the *kuruma-gaeshi ue* fashion.

(3) UKETACHI: withdraw the right foot and block the *sune* strike.

(4) SHIDACHI: step forward with the right foot and strike *shōmen* in the *kuruma-gaeshi shita* fashion.

(4) UKETACHI: step backward with the left foot and block the *shōmen* strike with the *shinogi*.

(5) SHIDACHI: step forward with the left foot and perform a *harai-otoshi* to the right on the *tachi* with the shaft.

(5) UKETACHI: receive the *harai-otoshi* on your left.

(6) SHIDACHI: step forward from the left foot and thrust with the *ishizuki* to the right flank. [although described on the next to last picture, the action of assuming *hassō* in order to gather momentum before the final thrust is not written in the guidelines]

(6) UKETACHI: take a step back from the left foot.

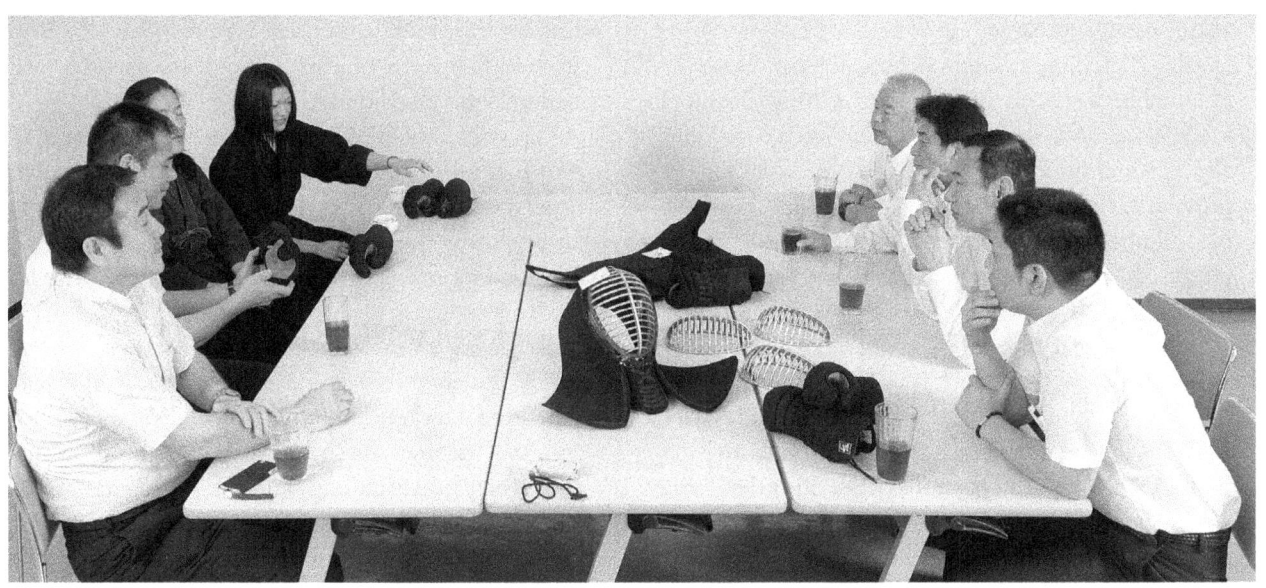

BOGU REVOLUTION
The "Antimicrobial Bogu" for Comfortable and Hygienic Keiko!

Discussion participants (Right side, front to rear): Mr. Hayashi Takahiro (Tozando), Mr. Kimura Takahiko (President of Tozando), Mr. Takai Nobuaki (Chairman of Taikai Budogu Co.,Ltd), Mr. Kaminakamura Susumu (Budoshop Factory Director). **(Left side, front to rear)** Prof. Kōda (Head Instructor of Tsukuba University Kendo Club), Prof. Arita (Coach of Tsukuba University Kendo Club), Ms. Kyo (Research Student at Tsukuba University), Ms. Kōsaka (Tsukuba University fourth-year student).

As we all know, bōgu parts absorb sweat during keiko which then causes it to produce bacteria and an unpleasant smell, a problem that becomes more serious in the extremely hot and humid Japanese summers. In order to try and combat the problem of unpleasant smelling bōgu, Tozando released a new range of "BioCLEAN" products in the summer of 2012, which have some ingenious antimicrobial properties. Tozando asked members of the kendo club at Tsukuba University, one of Japan's strongest kendo universities, to try these new BioCLEAN products and then give feedback.

Hayashi: I have been doing kendo since I was in junior high school, and the bad odour of *bōgu* has always been a problem. To begin the conversation today, I would like to ask for a female's point of view on the problem of 'smelly' *bōgu*.

Kōsaka: In my high school days, other people would often comment on the smell of *bōgu*. I noticed it myself whenever I wore my *men*. I tried to eliminate the smell by putting soap in my *kote* after *keiko*. However, even though the soap was perfumed, it got mixed in with the smell of my *bōgu* which created a stronger odour. Another headache with using soap was that the inside of my *kote* became slimy when mixed with sweat, and my hands became wrinkled. It was horrible.

Kōda: Wiping the sweat away and then drying the *men* in the shade after every practice can reduce the smell. This works, but few people actually do it.

Kōsaka: At Tsukuba University, we have a drying room especially for the kendo club. We put our *bōgu* there when *keiko* ends, but the smell is always there.

Arita: I sweat a lot, so I appreciate the fact that we have a drying room at my workplace. But, I know that the bad smell is one of the main reasons people don't like kendo sometimes.

Kyo: Ten years ago, I started kendo in New York. Every year, we had women come along who wished to start kendo, but after one or two weeks passed they quit because of the smell.

Kimura: It really is a pity when a person is interested in kendo and visits a dojo, but he or she then decides not to join just because of the smell of *bōgu*. If we could solve this problem, I am sure that the kendo population would grow.

Kōda: We are teaching kendo in regular physical education classes at school now. The problem is that *bōgu* used in a first period class is also used in the second period by different students. It is really unpleasant for the students, and many choose not to do kendo for their elective class again because of that.

Hayashi: Even though budo has been made compulsory in junior high schools from this year, I think that most schools use *bōgu* that is in an unsanitary condition. *Bōgu* with antimicrobial properties is essential for the popularisation of kendo. Tozando asked members of Tsukuba University's kendo club to try our newly released BioCLEAN products. What are your impressions?

Kōsaka: I felt that the sweat did not seep into the *kote* as much.

Kyo: Usually, the inside of *kote* becomes soft after *keiko*, and then hard when it dries. However, since the BioCLEAN *kote* is soft from the outset, I felt that I was able to grip the *shinai* well.

Kimura: Toray's "Sillead", which has great fast-drying and antibiotic properties, is used for the parts that directly touch the skin. Antimicrobial fabric by Teijin (usually used in hospitals) is used for the core material. Also, Toray's antimicrobial artificial leather is used for the surface. This structure prevents bacteria from growing even if sweat reaches the surface. The biggest difference between BioCLEAN and other *bōgu* that claim to have antimicrobial properties is that our *bōgu* is immersed in a special antibacterial solvent (made with silver ion) in the final stage of its production. This is to infuse the antimicrobial agents into the *bōgu*. Next, the *bōgu* is dried in a machine using infrared rays.

Takai: It has been 40 years since I started creating *mengane*, and more than 100 years if I include my father's generation. I often receive requests from all over Japan to repair *mengane*, and I have noticed that the part of *mengane* in front of the mouth becomes rusty from an accumulation of spit. It is natural to spit when you exert yourself in *keiko*, but I have always wanted to solve this problem as it breeds bacteria and fungus. Therefore, I coated the *mengane* with an antimicrobial agent which sterilizes spit when it comes into contact with the metal.

Kimura: With Mr. Takai, we tried several antimicrobial materials and finally found that silver ion has the most lasting effect on metal and fibre. It has taken five years of research to reach this conclusion. Silver ion is also used in hospitals on medical appliances.

Takai: In tests we have found that the bacteria will not grow even after one or two years.

Hayashi: To make sure that the *bōgu* is fast-drying, we used Sillead and manufactured it with the "Micro-Punch" method for the inside and outside of the *kote*. This is the main feature of our new BioCLEAN Dry Mesh Kote.

Kaminakamura: The difficult thing in its manufacture was gluing Sillead onto the futon as it is quite a soft, shiny material. Also, it was also hard to manufacture the parts for the inside and outside of the *kote* where the Micro-Punch mesh is used.

Kimura: We tested the inside leather many times to make sure it won't rip easily. This is the part that Mr. Kaminakamura paid particular attention to.
As for safety, the BioCLEAN *mengane* has horizontal bars that are set at the base at a right-angle. It requires an advanced technique to produce this type of *mengane*. In a typical *bōgu* the angle is slightly skewed, but this is not good for reducing impact. This is not the case with our new *mengane*.

Takai: *Mengane* used to be made of iron or nickel silver. To make lighter *mengane* duralumin or titanium ones have been developed in recent years. However, when a *mengane* becomes too light, it does not absorb impact well. Therefore, we mixed both the advantages of iron and duralumin in what we call the "IBB Mengane". "IBB" means "Ideal Best Balance". Soft iron is only used in the part that is hit by *shinai*. Since the centre of gravity is different from a regular *mengane*, it fits better on the head, and you do not feel the weight as much. The new *mengane* we developed for this *bōgu* is called the "IBB BioCLEAN" which took us and Tozando five years to develop.

Kimura: I asked Mr. Takai to create specific *mengane* for women and children. By the end of this year, we will be finishing the children's model, "BioCLEAN Junior", and also the women's model. Also, we are producing *tezashi* (hand-stitched) *bōgu* as well.

Kōda: How about creating odour free *kendō-gi* and *hakama*?

Kimura: Just bring them to us and we will make them BioCLEAN. We can wash them using a special method and immerse them into BioCLEAN solution.
The big problem that facilitates bacteria and smelly *bōgu* is the way that it is dried. A typical drying method cannot kill bacteria in the central core of the futon, which is the source of the bad smell. We use a special infrared ray machine, one usually used in hospitals to dry beds, to dry *bōgu*. This machine kills all the bacteria in the core of the material. Then we treat it with BioCLEAN solution.
In addition, this silver ion fabric has high washing protection so that the effect will not be diminished much after numerous washes. We are also producing Bio-Cleaned *himo* and are planning to develop Bio-Cleaned *bōgu* bags and *tsuka-gawa* as well. I do believe that to promote kendo, it is very important to offer *bōgu* that is assured for safety and usability with cleanliness provided via an antimicrobial action. Manufacturers like us must make efforts to maintain and help grow the kendo population. I think that contributing to the evolution of *bōgu* such as enhancing hygienic attributes will play a part in this.

See the following link:
http://www.tozandoshop.com/IBB_BioCLEAN_Ultimate_Hygenic_Fit_stitched_Bog_p/set1001.htm

www.ingramcontent.com/pod-product-compliance
Lightning Source LLC
Chambersburg PA
CBHW080856090426
42735CB00014B/3166